# GARY
# PLAYER

# GARY PLAYER

## GOLF'S GLOBAL AMBASSADOR

FROM SOUTH AFRICA TO AUGUSTA

# JOHN BOYETT

With photography from the *Augusta Chronicle*
and Black Knight International Archives

Charleston          London

THE
History
PRESS

Published by The History Press
Charleston, SC 29403
www.historypress.net

Copyright © 2012 by John Boyette
All rights reserved

Cover photo by Jonathan Ernst, *Augusta Chronicle*.

First published 2012

Manufactured in the United States

ISBN 978.1.60949.621.0

Library of Congress CIP data applied for.

*To Seve Ballesteros and all the international champions
who were inspired by Gary Player*

# Contents

# Acknowledgements

As a student of golf history, and the Masters Tournament in particular, I thought I knew pretty much everything I needed to know about Gary Player. As it turns out, I was wrong.

When I began this project, I knew the basic facts about his career and his many accomplishments. But I didn't realize the full scope of the difficulties he faced not only as a competitor but as one of South Africa's most recognized figures.

I think Gary Player is one of those rare people who transcends the sport he helped popularize and grow into what it is today. His true legacy one day might not be his amazing golf career. It could very well be his devotion to health and fitness or his humanitarian efforts around the globe.

This book came together very quickly, and I would like to acknowledge several people for their help and assistance.

First, I would like to thank the Player family for their time. Gary, Vivienne and Marc all made themselves available for interviews. Each of them added greatly to the story I was trying to tell.

Guy DeSilva, business development and media director for the Gary Player Group, deserves a special thank-you. He patiently answered all my questions and helped arrange interviews with the Player family. Plus, he helped provide many of the photographs found in this book.

Debbie Longenecker and Scott Ferrell, two key employees in the Player organization, also were very gracious and helpful.

Getting a book published is no small task, and I'd like to thank the folks at The History Press for their assistance. Adam Ferrell, Jessica Berzon and many others were instrumental in getting this book into print.

At the *Augusta Chronicle*, I'd like to thank my bosses, Alan English and John Gogick, for their support. Sean Moores also did his usual great job in assisting me with photos. Our sports columnist, Scott Michaux, also contributed some information that was of great help. The publisher of the *Chronicle*, William S. Morris III, also deserves my thanks. It was he who suggested I look into doing a book on Gary Player for my next project.

And finally, a big thanks to my family: my wife, Kathy, Mom, Dad and my sister, Angela. You'll never know how much your support and encouragement have meant through the years.

# Introduction

April 11, 1974.

The date of my first trip to Augusta National Golf Club and the Masters Tournament is etched in my brain forever. I was eight years old, and I had never seen grass that green or a gathering of people that large. I didn't quite understand what all the fuss was about.

I had never swung a golf club, and no one in my family was a regular player. But my grandparents, Estelle and Andy, got Masters badges each year. My father and I were allowed to use them on that Thursday, the first round of the tournament.

One slight problem: my mother was in the hospital giving birth to my sister that day. Angela Renee Boyette came into the world that morning, and then my father and I took off for the Masters. I'm not sure that was the right decision, but I don't think Mom holds it against us. She's a sports fan and understands the value of a Masters badge.

I don't have many memories of that day, but I do recall my father pointing out some of the top golfers. One of them was a slender man, and I believe he was wearing all black. It turned out to be Gary Player, and three days later, the South African won his second Masters with a clutch shot on the seventeenth hole in the final round.

I took up golf in the summer of 1980, and before long, I was making regular trips to the Masters each spring. As a member of the USC–Aiken college golf team, I got to work on the leader board at No. 6 in 1984 and 1985. The following year, having already begun my journalism career as a part-time writer at the *Aiken Standard*, I got to help cover the Masters for the first time. I followed Jack Nicklaus around the course in the final round, and of course he shot sixty-five to win in one of the most thrilling golf tournaments of all time. I was hooked.

I continued to cover the Masters each year, and in 1996, I left the *Standard* for a copy editor's position at the *Augusta Chronicle*. For two years I helped with our Masters coverage from the inside, but in 1998, sports editor Ward Clayton recruited me to help with the reporting from the course. When Ward left two years later, I was promoted to sports editor.

This will be my twelfth year of directing our newspaper's award-winning coverage, and it is a thrill and pleasure to be part of such a dedicated team. Most people think the greatest perk of my job is getting to play Augusta National each year in the media outing—and it probably is—but a close second would be the access I have to the greatest golfers in the world, past and present. When it comes to the Masters, the *Augusta Chronicle* and its reputation carries a lot of weight and opens a lot of doors.

Such was the case in 2003, when I had my first big interview with Gary Player. He was celebrating his fiftieth year as a professional, and I had arranged for a phone interview with him. But that also was around the time that Augusta National and Masters chairman Hootie Johnson had tried to phase out the lifetime invitation for former champions, and Gary was none too pleased about it.

Fortunately, Chairman Johnson relented, and Player was free to play as long as he wished. He matched Arnold Palmer with his fiftieth appearance in 2007, and for good measure he added two more Masters to set a record that might never be broken.

When I approached Player's people about this book last summer, I had no inkling that he was about to be invited to join Palmer and Nicklaus as honorary starters. He is certainly deserving of that honor, and what a treat it will be to see the Big Three again on the first tee in Augusta.

When I interviewed Player at his design headquarters in Travelers Rest, South Carolina, he looked about the same as when I first saw him some four decades earlier: trim, fit and dressed in all black but with touches of silver showing. A recent trip to the doctor had given him pause for concern, but that didn't stop him from giving me a lengthy interview and a chance to give me his views on everything from golf to politics to health and fitness.

The next day, when I returned for more interviews with his family, Player had returned from a trip to the gym. Six decades of travel hasn't slowed him down a bit. He stopped to point out one of the framed photos that showed him finishing a swing. He asked if my follow-through looked like his did in his prime. I assured him it didn't.

Player is no longer a regular competitor on any tour, and he is nearly fifteen years removed from his last major victory. But he still knows a lot about life and golf, and he enjoys imparting his wisdom wherever he goes.

I hope you enjoy learning about Gary Player's career as much as I did, and I hope you learn some lessons beyond golf as well. I know I certainly did.

Chapter 1

# Pass the Hat

G ary Player can sit back at his headquarters in South Carolina and admire a collection of trophies that no golfer—past or present—can claim. Not only did Player win the career Grand Slam on the regular tour, but he added the Senior Grand Slam as well. Those eighteen combined major victories in golf's most important events are only a small part of what defines Player. Now seventy-six, he has amassed an empire that includes a thriving course design business, numerous sponsorship deals and a business with offices around the globe.

Not bad for a man who comes from such humble origins. Player said:

> *It's a gift from God. It's called "it." You can never describe it. I've played with golfers that were better than me, and yet when it came to the majors, I beat them and won far more. I see the only trophies on this planet, the regular Grand Slam and the international Grand Slam, and I'm the only one who's ever done it. If I start taking the credit now, I'm crazy. It's all a gift. It's a loan. How did I do it? But I did it.*

You could hardly say that Gary Jim Player's upbringing was conducive to becoming one of golf's all-time greatest champions. While many players receive private instruction at an early age and continue to learn at college before turning professional, Player had no such luxuries. Just surviving on his own was an everyday challenge for Player, who was born in Johannesburg, South Africa, on November 1, 1935. The United States was in the midst of the Great Depression, Europe was on the brink of war and life wasn't very easy for Player, either. His description of his childhood is succinct:

> *Mother's dead when you're eight, and your father's working in a gold mine twelve thousand feet underground. Your brother's fighting alongside the Americans in the last world war at seventeen years of age. My sister's in boarding school, and I come home to a little crummy house. An hour and twenty minutes to get home, by streetcar and bus, and there's no one there at a dark house. Not easy. You leave at 5:30 in the morning, get dressed, cook your own breakfast, travel to school on your own, eight years old, that's tough. Nobody to help you.*

Player would later draw from those experiences whenever he got in a tough spot in a golf tournament, and he would go on to win 165 tournaments worldwide and reach heights that few in his sport ever achieved.

But golf was not his first love. Team sports captured his fancy early on, according to his wife, Vivienne. "My father was a golf professional. Gary's father was a very good single handicap player," she said. "So he was anxious for Gary to play golf, but he was more interested in school sports. Swimming and diving, and so on. He agreed to come out to the club where my dad was pro, and that's how we met and started playing golf together."

His father finally convinced him to tag along for a round. "I parred the first three holes I played," Player once said. "The rest of them were eights and nines, but I was absolutely, completely hooked."

Player was smitten with both the attractive young woman and the game of golf. He took up the sport when he was fourteen, and through hard work and practice, he became a scratch player in sixteen months. Upon graduation from high school, he went to work for Vivienne's father, Jock, as an assistant at the Virginia Park course.

He turned professional in 1953 when he was just seventeen, and success was not far off. He won the Egyptian Match Play and the East Rand Open in 1955 for the first of his many triumphs. But he was far from a wealthy man. He and Vivienne were still dating, and to marry her, he needed more money.

Traveling to Australia to play in the Ampol Tournament in 1956, Player made a bold proclamation: "If I win, I will marry Vivienne immediately." The tournament featured the largest purse in golf outside the United States.

Gary Player is all smiles as he arrives home in South Africa. With more than fifteen million miles of air travel, Player is considered the world's most-traveled athlete. *Courtesy of Black Knight International Archives.*

A few days later, Player did win the tournament. True to his word, he sent a cable to his future bride: "We've won 5,000 [pounds] and will marry immediately."

Vivienne received the news at the Maccauviel golf course, and she was overcome with joy. A photograph of her celebrating won a prize for news photo of the year in South Africa. She said she was "the happiest girl in South Africa."

Player's big win capped an important year for him. He also had won three other events in 1956, and he had made his major championship debut with a solo fourth at the British Open.

While Player and his bride-to-be were planning their wedding for the following year, Player's father, Harry, also had some big plans. With his son's growing résumé, he felt it was time for him to venture to the United States and test his game against the best in the world.

Harry Player wrote Augusta National chairman Clifford Roberts a letter in 1956. In it, he outlined his son's growing list of accomplishments. It also included this: "But if you could extend him an invitation to the Masters, I will pass the hat here in Johannesburg and obtain the necessary funds."

The response from Augusta was concise and included three words that would help launch Player's career: "Pass the hat."

Player was married in January 1957, and a couple months later, he made the journey to Augusta. He was one of just eleven international players in the select field. A new challenge awaited players in Augusta that spring: a thirty-six-hole cut would be made for the first time and would pare the field to the low forty and ties. Player struggled to an opening round of 77 but bounced back with an even-par 72 to make the cut, which fell at 150, by 1 stroke.

On the weekend, Player posted rounds of 75 and 73 to finish tied for twenty-fourth. His 297 total was nowhere near Doug Ford's winning score of 283, but it did earn Player $700.

Esteemed golf writer Herbert Warren Wind wrote that he first saw Player in 1957 and that he "was terribly disappointed." "He had an ugly swing, for he was intent on hitting the golf ball as far as the big men did, and in his pursuit of length he set up in an overly wide stance, wrapped the club around his neck going back, and practically jumped at the ball at impact," Wind wrote in the *New Yorker*. "Nevertheless, he contrived to bring in some surprisingly good scores, for he used the wedge well and putted like an angel."

In short order, Player would correct those flaws. While he continued to regularly win in South Africa and Australia, Player collected his first tournament victory in the United States at the 1958 Kentucky Derby Open.

Wind wrote that he "barely recognized" Player's swing when he saw him in 1958. "He now had a good-looking orthodox American-type swing, and he hit the ball nicely and far," Wind wrote.

While he missed the cut that year at the Masters, Player finished second at the U.S. Open and seventh at the British Open. He clearly had the talent to win the biggest events, and he didn't have to wait very long for his first breakthrough.

In 1959, Player claimed his first major championship. It came at the British Open at Muirfield. The South African opened with seventy-five but improved with rounds of seventy-one and seventy. Still, he was full of confidence that he could win.

Playing well ahead of the leaders, Player posted one of the final round's best scores. All he needed was a par four on the final hole to complete a fine round of sixty-six. Instead, a wayward drive found a bunker, and it took an extra shot to reach the green. He three-putted for a double bogey six and left the green disconsolate, certain that he had thrown away the Open.

But the leaders behind him faltered, and Player and his wife received word in their hotel room that he was needed at the closing ceremony. A claret jug with Gary Player's name on it was waiting.

At twenty-three, Player had made quite a mark on the game of golf in a short period. Not many could have predicted that he was about to leave his imprint all over the world, including Augusta.

Chapter 2

# Dethroning the King

It was no secret that Bobby Jones and Clifford Roberts, the men who co-founded Augusta National Golf Club and the Masters Tournament, wanted a foreign-born player to win their tournament. They realized how important it would be not only to promote interest in the Masters but to help grow the game around the world as well.

Jones and Roberts, though, had several obstacles to overcome when the first Augusta National Invitation Tournament was held in 1934. First, getting players to make an overseas journey that was costly and time-consuming was not an easy sell, even if you did have one of the game's immortals in Jones as host. And second, there weren't a lot of top-notch international players to choose from in those days. Golfers from the British Isles had dominated the sport before and after the turn of the twentieth century, with players such as Harry Vardon, Ted Ray and Willie Anderson. But by the 1920s, the tide had turned for the United States, with Jones, Walter Hagen and Gene Sarazen leading the way.

So when Jones held his first spring gathering at Augusta National, the field of seventy-eight included a whopping four international players. Three were professionals from England, and one was a Canadian amateur. None finished better than a tie for forty-third.

Harry "Lighthorse" Cooper was one of those three English pros to compete in the first Masters. He withdrew after three rounds that year but tied for twenty-fifth the following year. He finished as runner-up in 1936 and 1938.

With World War II looming in Europe in the late 1930s, tournament golf took a back seat around the world. The Masters played on through 1942, just a few months after the Pearl Harbor attack, but the small field of forty-two golfers included just one international player.

When the Masters resumed in 1946, no foreigners were in the field at all. But that began to change the following year when South Africa's Bobby Locke made his first appearance at Augusta, and others began to follow. Argentina's Roberto de Vicenzo, Australia's Peter Thomson and Canada's Stan Leonard all made their presences felt in the 1950s.

By the time Gary Player made the arduous trek from South Africa to Augusta in the spring of 1957, Americans were clearly dominating the game everywhere except the British Open. Player's first four Masters appearances from 1957 to 1960 yielded little for him, as his debut coincided with Arnold Palmer's ascension. Player had a pair of top-ten finishes in 1959 and 1960, but he had yet to break seventy at Augusta National and had not really contended.

That all changed in 1961. Player and Palmer were the hottest players in golf when April arrived, and most folks expected the two to go toe-to-toe. Palmer was the defending champion and the most popular player in the game. Player was the leading money winner on the U.S. pro circuit coming into the Masters. And the two didn't disappoint: Palmer opened with sixty-eight and sixty-nine, and Player started with sixty-nine and sixty-eight. Through thirty-six holes, the two were dead even and four shots clear of their closest pursuer.

The Masters did not pair leaders according to scores in those days, so Palmer went off a few groups in front of Player in Saturday's third round. By the time Player reached the first tee, he was already two behind, as Palmer had birdied his first two holes. Not to be outdone, Player matched Palmer's start with birdies on his first two holes as well.

"I was shocked to see Palmer's start," Player admitted to reporters following his round. "But I was proud of that birdie at No. 1. That gave me a lift."

Player opened up some breathing room with his sixty-nine in the third round, while Palmer stumbled to seventy-three. But Player knew that even four shots wasn't much against a player like Palmer, whose go-for-broke style had won him two previous Masters titles. In 1958, Palmer made an eagle on the thirteenth while waiting for a ruling to ignite his run to his first major victory. In 1960, Palmer birdied his final two holes to snatch the green jacket from Ken Venturi.

In Sunday's final round, it looked as if Palmer might charge to victory again and become the first back-to-back champion at the Masters. Playing in a steady rain, Palmer was able to cut the four-shot deficit in half. Both men had started play on the final nine holes when Masters officials declared conditions unplayable and stopped play at 3:31 p.m.

"I would rather be two shots behind with nine to play than four shots back with 18 to play," Palmer told reporters. "But that's the way it is and they couldn't do anything else but call it off."

Player conceded that the washout might have given him a slight advantage. "I was quite happy about it," he said. "It was the only fair thing to do."

With the fourth round rescheduled for Monday, the pairings were kept the same for the final round. Player went off with Paul Harney at 1:31 p.m., and Palmer was matched with amateur Charlie Coe three groups later.

Both men played flawless golf on the first nine holes. Player again birdied the first two holes and then reeled off seven pars in a row to make the turn in two-under-par thirty-four. Palmer did him one better, picking up birdies at Nos. 2, 6 and 8, and his thirty-three trimmed the South African's lead to three. Player cracked first, making a bogey at the tenth, but he regained his composure and made pars at the eleventh and twelfth holes. Palmer, meanwhile, made par at the tenth to pick up another shot.

Twenty-four hours after Sunday's play was washed out, Player and Palmer were in virtually the same position as they had been the day before. Player came to the thirteenth hole in need of a birdie to keep pace with, or maybe push ahead of, Palmer. But the South African couldn't believe what he was seeing after he pushed his drive on the thirteenth hole into the pine trees lining the right side of the fairway.

The most polite gallery in all of golf—patrons at the Masters Tournament—wouldn't budge. Normally a birdie hole, or even a chance to get an eagle with two well-struck shots, the par-five thirteenth at Augusta National was built for drama. The decision of whether or not to go for the water-guarded green was one that every Masters champion had to face at some point in the tournament.

But that wasn't the dilemma facing Player. His poor drive had left him no choice but to lay up, but where? He had an opening that would allow him to play into the adjacent fourteenth fairway, but that's where the gallery was standing.

"I'd drove into the trees on the right, and I had a nice gap to go up 14 fairway. Which would have meant I'd only have had sand wedge into the green," Player said. "I couldn't get the people to move. [Jack] Nicklaus would have sat there until the people moved. Or Tiger [Woods]. But I'm a young man from South Africa and I don't want to be forceful."

The irony isn't lost on Player. One of the nicest players in the game was being done in by one of the game's best-behaved galleries. He could wait, or he could take a different route. The Masters was already running behind, and Player might have been a tad impatient.

"I'll just chip it back to the fairway," Player remembers thinking. "Of course it's downhill and trickles into the creek. A chip shot. And I get seven."

With five holes to go, Player's chance to become the first international champion in Masters history was slipping away.

No foreign-born player had ever won the Masters, and the pro-Palmer gallery was happy to keep it that way. After all, this was 1961, and Palmer was the king of golf and the Masters. The "Pennsylvania strong boy," as the American press liked to call him, was nearing the height of his popularity. With his powerful swing and rugged good looks, Palmer was the closest thing to a movie star on the links. The soldiers from Augusta's army base composed the first platoon of "Arnie's Army," and they weren't shy about voicing support for their hero.

So it was not a total surprise that Player couldn't get the gallery to cooperate when he reached the ball at the thirteenth. After driving into the trees on the right, Player began to unravel.

"[Player] hit a horrible second shot into Rae's Creek from there. After dropping out, he hit his next on the fringe and three-putted from 35 feet," Johnny Hendrix wrote in the *Augusta Chronicle*.

Now tied with Palmer, Player made a par on the fourteenth. He laid up short of the water at the par-five fifteenth, but his third shot spun back off the front of the green. He chipped close but missed the par putt.

Player would pick up no more ground. He made pars at the sixteenth and seventeenth, and he pushed his approach shot to the eighteenth hole into the right bunker. He played out to five feet and holed that for par and a total of 8-under 280. "As he signed his scorecard and walked off the course, Player was almost in tears," Alfred Wright wrote in *Sports Illustrated*.

Palmer kept chugging along with par after par, and he was one shot clear of Player heading into the final few holes. Palmer's playing partner, the amateur Coe, was creeping into contention. He made birdie at the thirteenth but missed an eagle putt at the fifteenth.

All Player and his wife, Vivienne, could do was watch and wait. After signing his scorecard, the South Africans went to the clubhouse to watch

Gary Player blasts out of the bunker on the final hole of the 1961 Masters. Player saved his par and went on to victory when Arnold Palmer, playing out of the same bunker, wasn't as successful and made a double bogey. *Courtesy of Black Knight International Archives.*

Palmer play the final three holes alongside Clifford Roberts. The forty on the final nine weighed heavily on Player's shoulders.

Palmer arrived at the eighteenth tee with his one-shot lead and a chance to make Masters history. A fine drive left him in the fairway, but like Player before him, he dumped his seven-iron second shot into the right-hand bunker.

Not wasting any time, Palmer bladed his bunker shot across the green. The gallery could hardly believe what it was seeing. Palmer's ball had run away from the green and toward a TV tower. Now, the reigning champion needed to sink this fourth shot if he was going to win outright. He chose a putter and hit the ball a little too firm, and it settled some fifteen feet past the hole. Now he needed to make this bogey putt to force a tie with Player. But Palmer missed, and the Masters had a new champion.

"That was the only shot I took any time on the eighteenth hole, and by that time it was too late," Palmer said of his bogey putt. Inexplicably, Palmer had rushed his way through the eighteenth hole. "I never thought for one minute that I was not going to win. I had a one-shot lead, but I kinda forgot you have to finish," he said.

The first international champion was gracious in his post-victory remarks, and he sympathized with Palmer's misfortune. "I'm very fond of Arnold. All I can say is tough luck," Player said. "I know you will win this many more times."

The national press placed much of its attention on Palmer's collapse at the final hole, but Player said *Sports Illustrated* was "very fair" in its coverage. "They wrote Gary won the tournament. He got a seven at thirteen, it doesn't matter which hole you get your double bogey on," Player said. "It was really a frustrating thing [thirteen]. I could have birdied the hole, which would have made a massive difference. It just goes to show you've got to have patience and you've got to make the right decisions. And mine was a terrible decision."

On the twenty-fifth playing of the Masters, Bobby Jones and Clifford Roberts finally had their international champion. And although they couldn't have realized it at the time, Jones and Roberts could not have asked for a better global representative.

Player touted the wonders of Augusta and the Masters wherever he traveled. And slowly but steadily, the number of international players increased. The numbers really began to increase in the 1990s, and now it is not unusual for more than half the Masters field to come from outside the United States.

Player would add two more Masters wins to his résumé, in 1974 and 1978, but it was not until 1980 that he would see a fellow international player win at Augusta. When Seve Ballesteros won the first of his two Masters titles, he was quick to give credit to Player. After all, he had been paired with the South African in the final round of 1978 when Player charged to victory.

"Gary Player is a very good friend of mine," Ballesteros said then. "He's not an American player, but he has more merit than any other.

"You always learn things from a superstar, especially how to fight," Ballesteros continued. "I played with Player many times and I learned from him a lot."

Player visited the media center in 2011 to discuss the fiftieth anniversary of his breakthrough win. "Obviously when you are finished and you sit down and you think about this tournament, you say to yourself, well, you're the first international player to win," Player said. "Let's hope that this will continue in this vein and that we'll have other players who now believe that they can come along and do it. And so that's happily happened.

"I had to write it down because there are so many of them," Player said as he recited the names of his fellow international champions. "They all came along and went after me, and it's wonderful to know that you gave people the confidence to come along and do it."

# THE GREEN JACKET

The green jacket has been the symbol of Augusta National and the Masters almost since the beginning of the tournament. Members began wearing the jackets, originally made by Brooks Uniform Co. of New York, in 1937. They were encouraged to wear them so that patrons could readily identify a person who was knowledgeable about the tournament.

In 1949, the club awarded a green jacket to the Masters winner for the first time. Sam Snead, who won the first of his three Masters victories that spring, was the first champion to slip into the green coat.

Protocol calls for the green jackets to be kept at the club and worn only on the Augusta National's grounds. That applies to members and the current champion, who is permitted to keep it for his year as winner and then bring it back the following year.

Gary Player kisses his wife, Vivienne, after slipping on the green jacket at the 1961 Masters. *Courtesy of the* Augusta Chronicle.

But Gary Player didn't know that, or at least that was his explanation. After losing a playoff in 1962 to Arnold Palmer, he packed the jacket and took it to his home in South Africa. That led to a call from Clifford Roberts, who was a stickler for club rules.

"I didn't know you were supposed to leave it there," Player said. "Next thing you know, there was a call from Mr. Roberts."

According to Player, here's how the exchange went:

> *"Gary, have you got the jacket?"*
> I said, *"Yes, I do."*
> He said, *"Well, no one ever takes the jacket away from here."*
> And I said, *"Well, Mr. Roberts, if you want it, why don't you come and fetch it?"*

Roberts, who didn't lose many arguments, agreed to a compromise. "He kind of chuckled and said don't wear it in public," Player recounted.

Today, the very jacket that Player won in 1961 is on display at his design headquarters in Travelers Rest, South Carolina. The jacket and other Player memorabilia were appraised as a lot by auction house Christie's in 2003, but the items were never sold.

And, true to Player's word, the green jacket is not worn in public.

## Chapter 3

# A Wife's Perspective

If Gary Player is the most traveled athlete in the history of sports, then his wife must have logged a considerable amount of air miles, too. Vivienne Player hadn't considered that.

"I never thought about that. I'd like to see which golfing wives have traveled more than I have," she said. "In the early days, it was really tough traveling. But you do what you have to do. That's one of Barbara Nicklaus's lines."

Traveling from South Africa to Augusta in the 1950s and 1960s was not an easy journey. From Johannesburg, the flight would take the Player clan to a stop in Europe, say London or Paris. Then, they would change planes and board a flight to New York. From there, a flight to Atlanta or Augusta would complete the trip. The entire journey would often take more than forty hours.

While Player was focused on his golf and often was already in the United States, his wife would have to worry about traveling with a brood that would eventually grow to six children: Jennifer, Marc, Wayne, Michele, Theresa and Amanda. They also have twenty-one grandchildren.

"It was a major issue, traveling with small children. No disposable diapers. No great conveniences," she said. "I watch the mothers now, and they push their baby in a stroller to the door of the plane. They take the stroller from you and have it right there when you get off the plane. We didn't have anything like that. I think, 'Oh my gosh, how did I manage with six children?'"

Gary and Vivienne Player show off daughter Jennifer and baby Marc during a break in the action at the 1961 Masters. *Courtesy of the* Augusta Chronicle.

Of course, Vivienne Verweigh knew what she was getting into when she married Player. The daughter of a golf professional, she was a fine player in her own right.

Married in 1957, it wasn't long before Player was headed for the United States and the Masters Tournament. It was an exciting trip for both of them. "Oh, you hear about the Masters through the years," she said. "And when our pilot flew over Augusta, we could see the huge parking lots and green golf course, it was obviously exciting and thrilling. It never diminished, in fact. Each year when we went back, it was a thrill. It's beautiful, exciting, wonderful. You see so many friends from all over the world there."

The price for living in South Africa and traveling around the globe was a heavy one for Player. He was away from his family often and even missed the births of some of his children.

"We should have lived in America. He could have come home more," Vivienne Player said. "He didn't see his daughter [Jennifer] until she was three months old. In the meantime, he won the British Open. He traveled to Muirfield and he won the British Open. He wasn't with me when Marc was born. He brought Marc over as a one-month-old and he won the Masters. You look back and, yes, you make sacrifices, but it was worthwhile."

Player said being away from his children and grandchildren was the toughest challenge of his career. "It just breaks my heart. The times I've had to say goodbye, you can't see them, and you wish you live in the same neighborhood. People who have been married for a long time and have family who live in the same neighborhood just don't realize how lucky they are."

In nearly six decades of traveling, Player estimates that he has logged more than fifteen million miles. He said at the 2009 Masters that he is grateful to have such a good wife, one who accompanied him on many arduous trips. "My goodness, she's spoiled me and looked after me; never complained

Gary Player gets a kiss from wife Vivienne after winning the 1961 Masters. *Courtesy of the Augusta Chronicle.*

about going away, always continuously going by, raising six children," Player said. "You have to be lucky to have a wife like that."

Vivienne admits that both of them are starting to slow down their schedules. They enjoy spending time on their property in South Africa for part of the year, and they have a residence in south Florida.

"I think he's getting a bit tired of all the traveling, but he's a very good traveler," she said. "He's small and can curl up and sleep like a log for eight or ten hours. And I travel well and sleep very well. We're very healthy, which is a great blessing."

Chapter 4

# **Grand Slam**

Gary Player's first win at the Masters served as notice that he would be a force on the American pro circuit. Arnold Palmer might have still been the king, but Player wasn't going to back down.

When the two men returned to Augusta in 1962, they were the favorites once again. And with three holes to go, it looked like Player might be the first player to win green jackets in back-to-back years. But just as it had been with Palmer the year before, it was not to be.

"People often say what was the worst moment of your life in golf? And I say 1962," Player said.

Coming to the sixteenth hole of the final round, Player held a two-shot lead over Palmer. He said:

> *I put it twelve feet from the hole* [at sixteen]. *He misses the green to the right. Flag's down bottom left. You know you can't get it down in two from there. I said to my caddie, "We've won. We'll have a three-shot lead at the worst with two holes to go." Down the hill, with the big break.* [Player smacks his hands together.] *It hits the flag* [and goes in]. *Would have gone in the bunker.*

Palmer's good fortune continued at the next hole. Player said:

> *On seventeen he hit a big hook into the Eisenhower Tree and hits five-iron, I'll never forget that, twenty-five to thirty feet from the hole, and*

*he holed that. We tied and we meet in the playoff* [along with Dow Finsterwald]. *I shoot thirty-four on the front nine and he shot thirty-seven. At ten he hit a lousy shot to the right of the green, and I hit it right over the flag, and he holed that across the green and came back in thirty-one. So that was always the worst moment for me. But those things happen.*

Palmer's third Masters victory came at Player's expense, but the South African didn't let it get him down. With victories in the British Open and Masters for his career, Player was halfway to a career Grand Slam. All he needed was a PGA Championship and U.S. Open to complete professional golf's highest achievement.

But only two men had achieved the feat: Gene Sarazen and Ben Hogan. Sarazen won the second Masters in 1935 in dramatic fashion with a double eagle in the final round to force a playoff. He beat Craig Wood the next day in the only thirty-six-hole playoff in Masters history.

Hogan was a late bloomer who struggled with his swing early in his career. All nine of his major championships came after World War II, and his most impressive feat came after he was nearly killed in a car wreck in Texas. Hogan won golf's Triple Crown in 1953 with victories in the Masters, U.S. Open and British Open. The latter triumph gave him the British Open title he needed to complete the Grand Slam, and it would prove to be his final major triumph.

The odds were good that Palmer would be the next player to join the exclusive fraternity of Grand Slam champions. All he needed was a PGA Championship.

Two months after his 1962 Masters win, Palmer lost an eighteen-hole playoff to Jack Nicklaus at the U.S. Open. But he recovered the following month with a win at the British Open, his sixth major title in five years. Up next was the PGA, and like the U.S. Open at Oakmont, it was played in Palmer's home state of Pennsylvania. With his victory the week before at the British, Palmer would be a heavy favorite to capture that elusive major he needed to complete the Grand Slam.

Player wasn't a factor at the U.S. Open, and he missed the cut at the British. "I had left the British Open at Troon with my tail between my legs," Player told the *Philadelphia Inquirer*. Missing the cut gave him an edge over Palmer and the other pros: he would have plenty of time to become familiar with the Donald Ross–designed Aronimink in Newtown Square, Pennsylvania, and he could also prepare for the sweltering heat.

Gary Player won the 1962 PGA Championship at Aronimink Golf Club in Newtown Square, Pennsylvania. *Courtesy of Black Knight International Archives.*

Player opened with rounds of seventy-two and sixty-seven to trail thirty-six-hole leader Doug Ford by one stroke. A sixty-nine in the third round left Player all alone in first, but he wasn't particularly happy. "I never seem to play well when I'm ahead," he told reporters.

With Palmer out of contention and Nicklaus off to a slow start, Player's main challenge came from Bob Goalby. The South African built a big lead early, but Goalby kept whittling away, and when the American made birdies at fourteen and sixteen, the lead was down to one.

On the final hole, Player hit his tee shot to the right and didn't have a direct shot to the green. But the crafty Player figured out how to get his ball on the green to secure the victory. "The shot I hit at the last hole I will never forget," Player told the *Inquirer*. "I took a 3-wood and I aimed it 100 yards left of the green and hit the biggest slice around the corner and onto the green."

Player now claimed three of the four majors necessary for a Grand Slam, but the U.S. Open continued to be elusive for him. While all of the four majors have their own personalities, the U.S. Open is regarded as the toughest mental examination. The venues were classic courses that featured deep rough and slick greens, and the seventy-two holes were compressed into three days. The tournament ended on a Saturday with thirty-six grueling holes.

That practice came to an end in 1964, after Ken Venturi nearly succumbed to the conditions at Congressional Country Club in suburban Washington, D.C. Venturi needed medical supervision as he played the last day, but he managed to post rounds of sixty-six and seventy on the final day for his only major championship.

Player had become a fixture in the top ten of majors, but he had not won one since the 1962 PGA at Aronimink. He and Palmer tied for second at the 1965 Masters, but they weren't really close, as Nicklaus won by a whopping nine strokes.

With a new four-day format, the U.S. Open that year was held at Bellerive Country Club in St. Louis. The course measured nearly 7,200 yards and featured a handful of par-fours that were longer than 450 yards, but Player opened with a pair of seventies to take control of the tournament.

A seventy-one in the third round left Player ahead, and the tournament would come down to a battle between him and Kel Nagle. The Australian had derailed Arnold Palmer's bid for a Grand Slam in one year in 1960 when he beat him at the British Open.

With three holes to go, Player had what seemed to be an insurmountable lead of 3. But he promptly double bogeyed the par-three sixteenth, and Nagle rolled in his birdie putt at the seventeenth. Tied at 282, the two men headed for an eighteen-hole Monday playoff.

Gary Player reacts to sinking a putt during his victory in the 1965 U.S. Open. The win was the fourth major championship of his career and allowed him to complete the career Grand Slam. *Courtesy of Black Knight International Archives.*

"The playoff was anticlimactic," Robert Sommers wrote in his history of the U.S. Open. "Nagle's shots ran wild—twice he drove into the crowd and hit spectators—and Player rushed to a five-stroke lead after eight holes."

Player finished with seventy-one to Nagle's seventy-four, and the career Grand Slam was his. "Quite simply, I consider winning the Grand Slam as the finest achievement in my golfing career," Player would say years later.

To show his appreciation, Player then did something that was almost unheard of: he donated his entire check of $25,000 to charity. Of that, $5,000 was earmarked for cancer research in tribute to his mother, Muriel, who died of the disease, and the remaining $20,000 was handed over to Joe Dey, the U.S. Golf Association's executive director, to promote junior golf.

"I am doing this because I made a promise to Joe Dey and to repay America for its many kindnesses to me over the past few years," Player said.

# FASHION STATEMENT

Gary Player is well known for his all-black attire on the golf course, and it inspired his nickname of the Black Knight. But do you know its origin?

Player was a big fan of western movies and television shows, in particular *Have Gun—Will Travel* and Hopalong Cassidy. While most westerns depicted good guys wearing white hats and the bad guys in black, those shows were exceptions. The fictional Hopalong Cassidy, played by William Boyd, proudly wore black and was known as "the epitome of gallantry and fair play."

But it was Paladin, the character played by Richard Boone in the *Have Gun—Will Travel* series, who inspired Player the most. The fictional character was a gentleman gunfighter for hire who lived in San Francisco, and he was well read and a world traveler. His calling card included a chess knight symbol, and Player soon adopted a similar logo for his Black Knight brand.

The westerns also helped Player develop a love for horses. He started his own stud farm in South Africa, and it is now recognized for breeding some of the top Thoroughbreds in the world. Broadway Flyer, one of Player's horses, made it to the 1994 English Derby.

During his 1965 U.S. Open victory, Player recalls wearing the same black shirt each day of the tournament. Despite the searing heat of a St. Louis summer, Player wanted to keep wearing his "lucky" shirt and washed it each night by hand in his hotel room and put it on the shower rod to dry.

"A silly superstition, perhaps, but it gave me a certain level of karma," Player said in 2005.

Gary Player shows off the form that helped him win a combined 18 regular and senior majors and more than 160 golf tournaments around the world. *Courtesy of Black Knight International Archives.*

Chapter 5

# Mr. Fitness

When Ian Player left South Africa to go fight alongside the Americans in World War II, he left his younger brother with two things: a grim warning and a gift that would change his life. "He said, 'I might not come back,'" Gary Player said. "He said, 'Here are a couple of weights, I want you to exercise for the rest of your life.'"

Player took the message from his brother to heart and has been devoted to exercise and living a healthy lifestyle ever since. "I'm seventy-five now," he said at the 2011 Masters, "and I could beat 80 percent of the young boys off the street in a fitness contest today."

While today's generation of golfers is committed to staying fit and performing regular workouts, that concept was far from the norm when Player turned professional in the early 1950s. A golfer was more apt to hit the bar than the exercise room after the round in those days. Player was an exception. He always found time to get in his workouts, and he went against conventional thinking of the time that lifting weights would hurt your golf game.

When Player prepared to play in his fifty-second and final Masters in 2009, he repeated a story about how his fellow players viewed his exercise habit. "There was a famous man here, I won't mention his name, and he saw me when I was squatting with 325 pounds in the old YMCA," Player said. "He said, 'Can you imagine this man doing these weights? He'll never last thirty-five years.' When I won my tournament in '61, I said [looking up toward heaven], 'How are you up there? What's it like?'"

Gary Player defied conventional thinking and has lifted weights throughout his career. Even today, he still finds time for regular workouts in the gym. *Courtesy of Black Knight International Archives.*

While Player holds the record for Masters longevity—and no one is currently a threat to break it—he insists it will one day fall:

> *Oh, no, it will be broken. We are in our infancy when it comes to the mind and the body. They have a man in Canada, he weighs 165 pounds and he hit the ball 444 yards in the long driving competition. And we have not had the big men playing golf, the Michael Jordans and Shaquille O'Neals. They are coming, because they have seen Tiger. Tiger is playing a vital role. They are seeing this guy is making more money as he's going along and everyone else got to thirty and they were finished. So they are going to come into golf. We are going to see a lot of very interesting things.*

Player points to Woods as a prime example of how fitness and golf can mix successfully. He said in 2007:

> *I had to go to Abu Dhabi to bid on a golf course, and I went into Dubai and they were having the Dubai Desert Classic, and there was Tiger coming in the gym as I was leaving, and I said, "Good luck, Tiger."*
>
> *I turned around, finishing my exercises, and he was playing at one o'clock and he had these two twenty-five-pound dumbbells like they were five pounds* [lifting weights], *and he was playing. Now, if you do it excessively like he does, if you warm up with twenty-five-pound dumbbells, it seems a lot for the average person, but it's nothing like he normally does. So he's tuned his body to such a degree and he's such a phenomenal athlete and really deserves all of the success he gets with his work ethic.*

Player, though, is saddened that not everyone follows his example. He uses his pulpit as a top golfer to preach about fitness and warn about the consequences for those who don't follow a proper diet or exercise regularly. "Child obesity is one of the biggest problems facing America, maybe the biggest," he said. "I don't know how you're going to pay for all of this. It's doomed. You'll probably have 100 million Americans with diabetes in fifty years' time."

He places the blame on food. "Steroids, antibiotics, hormones…food is a massive problem," Player said. "One out of every three persons will get cancer. That's a frightening stat. I see the junk they feed children at school, and I see the junk that children eat. Where's the energy? Where's the productivity? How can you be a champion? How can you pay the medical bills?"

And he isn't shy about telling strangers, particularly if it involves a young person. He told *Golf Digest*:

> *Golf is the game for a lifetime, but that lifetime will be shorter if you're overweight. And while you're at it, encourage a young person to lose weight. Every week, I make a point of finding an overweight youngster in the gallery and taking his father aside. I tell these fellows, privately and very politely, "My son is a diabetic, and my father was a diabetic. When you get diabetes, you take insulin twice a day, and that doesn't stop it from affecting your eyes, your liver, your limbs and everything else. Please get your son on a good diet now." I think they're usually grateful.*

Part of his secret is that he has never smoked, and he limits his alcohol consumption to an occasional glass of wine. "There's no amount of money that would get me to smoke," he said. "My body is a holy temple. I've got an ambition to get across to billions of young people about your body. Stay fit. Be productive for your country. Stay well. It saves the government fortunes of money if you can stay fit."

In 2007, when Player matched Arnold Palmer with his fiftieth Masters appearance, he showed off his physique during a pre-tournament interview. When asked about his fitness routine, Player stood up and loudly slapped his firm stomach.

"I go into the gym and I do one thousand crunches and I do some with an eighty-pound weight," Player said of the routine he followed then five times a week. "I have to watch that my enthusiasm doesn't run away with me, but at seventy-one, I want you to see that I do those."

Chapter 6

# The Big Three

B y the mid-1960s, professional golf was dominated by Arnold Palmer, Gary Player and Jack Nicklaus. Collectively, the men were known as the Big Three, and not only did they win regularly, but they also had lucrative endorsements that supplemented their earnings on the course.

Credit for the creation of the Big Three goes to Mark McCormack, who founded International Management Group in 1960. A fine golfer in his own right, McCormack would become good friends with Palmer. As Palmer's career was taking off, he asked the attorney to represent his financial interests, and McCormack was wildly successful, as he had the golfer in a number of endorsements, appearances and licensing agreements.

Player and Nicklaus couldn't help but take notice of Palmer's success, and they soon joined IMG, with McCormack representing their interests as well. Before long, a television series was produced that featured the three men competing against one another.

But it was real competition on the course, especially at the majors, that really fired up Palmer, Player and Nicklaus. All three yearned to be the game's best, and nothing mattered more than winning the Masters, U.S. Open, British Open and PGA.

Palmer, the oldest of the trio, had the upper hand. By 1965, he had won seven majors. Player completed his career Grand Slam in 1965, and he had one win in each of the four majors. Nicklaus, who turned pro in 1962 after a stellar amateur career, also had four through 1965: two Masters, one U.S. Open and one PGA.

*From left*: Gary Player, Arnold Palmer and Jack Nicklaus are shown in Butler Cabin at the 1965 Masters. Nicklaus won the tournament, and Player and Palmer were runners-up. *Courtesy of the* Augusta Chronicle.

The Big Three's success at Augusta National was remarkable. From 1958, Palmer's first win there, through 1966, the men had won eight of the nine green jackets given annually to the winner. In a preview story for the 1966 Masters, *Sports Illustrated* ran an illustration of the three men and the green jacket on its cover. The magazine posed the question: was the Masters fixed so that only Palmer, Player and Nicklaus could win? "The Masters is hardly more in doubt than Batman's tussle with each week's guest villain," Gwilym S. Brown wrote.

Of course, the tournament wasn't fixed, but the Big Three's fellow professionals opined that the course favored their abilities. Three-time winner Jimmy Demaret said that the fairways should be narrowed. Billy Casper complained that the men had too much of an advantage on the par-fives.

Masters co-founders Clifford Roberts and Bobby Jones dismissed such talk. "When the obvious flukes and the unknowns begin winning the Masters is when we will begin wondering what is wrong with our golf course," Roberts said in the article.

Nicklaus would go on to win the 1966 Masters to become the first golfer to successfully defend his title. It capped an amazing run of success for the Big Three at Augusta. He added the British Open later that year to join Player in the select group of Grand Slam winners.

When they weren't butting heads at a major, the Big Three often traveled together for exhibitions and appearances. "We had a great camaraderie of friendship, which was great, and of course we wanted to beat each other," Player said. "We were great friends. We traveled around the world trying to promote golf."

Nicklaus reflected on his friendship with Palmer and Player when he turned seventy in 2010:

> *We had a lot of fun, we played a lot of places. Our wives were close friends. I always enjoyed the Big Three matches. We played all over the world. We opened up Mauna Kea in 1964* [in Hawaii], *and there was nothing there, the hotel hadn't started and we played a Big Three series of four matches. After the matches you would go down and jump in the ocean, the television crew and everybody was jumping in the ocean.*

In 1967, the Big Three traveled to Carnoustie to get a preview of the next year's British Open venue. Nicklaus said:

> *We went and it was a very windy day. Arnold shot seventy-nine and Gary shot seventy-eight and I shot seventy-six. We walked off there thinking it was the worst golf course we had ever seen, anywhere in the world. How in the world were we ever going to play the British Open there* [the next] *year?*
>
> *We got back, we were staying at a hotel in St. Andrews and were there with our wives that night, and Gary and I start looking at Arnold's round. Arnold had hit four greens in regulation and had twenty-five putts. We start giving Arnold the raspberries about it. As we were doing that, I started thinking about Gary's round. Gary had hit five greens in regulation and had twenty-six putts. Then it got to me and I had eight greens and had twenty-nine putts.*

The spirit of traveling together—and giving each other the needle—isn't found very often today. Nicklaus said:

*We had fun kidding each other. Through the years, we'd walk off the golf course, and we'd look at the scoreboard and if one of us shot seventy-four or seventy-five, we couldn't get to the locker room fast enough to say, "Hey, Arn, where did you get all your birdies today?" We had a good time. In the early years, Arnold and I played a ton of exhibitions together. He used to come to Columbus and pick me up in his Air Commander, and we'd go play a week of exhibitions together. We had a blast traveling all over the place. You don't do that today—guys just don't do that. We had a lot of fun, we got to know each other well and it was a real privilege to be able to do those things and to look back on them and say, "Hey, those were neat times."*

Palmer tells a similar tale of camaraderie in his book, *A Golfer's Life*:

*The competition was fierce, I must say, but so was the horsing around after the cameras finished shooting. I forget who started the friendly fracas the night after we finished shooting in Montreal, but you have it on good authority from me that Gary and Jack were always ganging up to try to beat me—even in a food fight!*

*Someone spilled a little ginger ale or champagne on somebody else, and soon corks were popping and bottles were fizzing and food of one kind or another was flying through the air. Poor Mark McCormack, who tried to hold the leash on all three of us, was none too pleased to receive the substantial cleaning bill from the hotel's management.*

As the end of the 1960s loomed, none of the Big Three could have predicted they would struggle to win majors. Palmer's final major came at the 1964 Masters, and after the 1966 season, Player and Nicklaus would win only one major apiece the rest of the decade.

While Nicklaus and Player would add to their major totals in the 1970s and 1980s, it wasn't long before the Big Three were battling it out on the course again. This time the stage was the Senior Tour, for golfers fifty and older, and Palmer helped launch the fledgling circuit when he joined in 1980. Other top players joined him when they became eligible, and that included Player and Nicklaus. The men were often grouped together in tournament play to attract galleries.

In 2000 and 2001, the Big Three went off together in the first two rounds of the Masters. While the crowds loved the chance to see the legends compete against one another on the big course, Nicklaus didn't care too much for the

*From left*: Arnold Palmer, Jack Nicklaus and Gary Player pose for a picture. The Big Three dominated golf in the 1960s and later competed against one another for course design jobs as well as on the Senior Tour. *Courtesy of Black Knight International Archives.*

pairing. According to Ian O'Connor's book *Arnie & Jack*, the Golden Bear felt he was being rushed into a ceremonial role.

Nicklaus outplayed the other two in 2000, shooting even par to make the cut before stumbling on the weekend. A year later, none of the Big Three made the cut, and the ceremonial grouping was done.

While the men made their reputations as rivals on the golf course, they also were fierce competitors in the business arena. That included

*From left*: Arnold Palmer, Jack Nicklaus and Gary Player pose after finishing their opening round in the 2000 Masters. It was the first time the three had been grouped together for a tournament round at the Masters. *Courtesy of the* Augusta Chronicle.

the golf course design business, and that is where the men staged some of their most competitive battles. Now, each man has more than three hundred design projects on his résumé.

While collaborations on golf courses between the men have been scarce, there is one unique course that features nine-hole designs by Palmer, Nicklaus and Player. Champions Retreat is located in the suburbs of Augusta. According to the club, Player recruited Palmer and Nicklaus to join him in the unique project during a Champions Dinner at Augusta National. The property borders the Savannah River, and Player designated the land into three areas: Island, Creek and Bluff. The three men drew index cards to see who would get which property, and Palmer went first because of his seniority. He picked Island. Nicklaus went second, and he came up with Bluff. That left Player with Creek. The course opened in 2005.

Despite their competitive natures and desire to be the best at whatever they were doing, the Big Three never lost sight of the big picture. Player said:

*We wanted to win, but at the same time, we had great respect for each other. We appreciated what we were trying to do, not just out there trying to make money. We were out there trying to promote the game of golf. We traveled to all corners of the globe not getting the millions of dollars and having your own jet and the conditions that they have today.*

*So it's very comforting, and I'm sure Arnold and Jack, if they were sitting here today, would have the same feeling that I have: that we tried to promote golf throughout the world.*

## Chapter 7
# Social Change

While the Big Three confined their battles to golf and business interests, the rest of the world wasn't as peaceful. In the United States, civil rights and the Vietnam War were hot issues that divided families and united protesters. In South Africa, apartheid—racial segregation—was an issue that was watched closely around the world. Apartheid began in 1948 when the National Party government came into power, and it greatly limited the rights of non-white inhabitants of South Africa. Schools, hospitals and other public services were segregated. For those who protested, it could mean imprisonment. Violence and uprisings were commonplace. In the early 1960s, Nelson Mandela, head of the African National Congress, was put in jail; he would serve twenty-seven years.

Gary Player was a compassionate man who wanted to help, but he felt his hands were tied. If he became outspoken, it could mean dire consequences for family and friends who lived in South Africa. In the 1960 British Open at St. Andrews, Player wore black and white pants to draw attention to his country's apartheid policies. But it was to no avail. He said in a 1993 interview:

> I had been brainwashed as a child in South Africa into believing that apartheid was "separate but equal," but then as a young pro, as I began to travel the world, I began to realize that things were not equal. At that point, I stopped supporting apartheid, but it is impossible for one man to change a country's policy overnight. Most of the world did not support

*America's involvement in the Vietnam War, but no protesters anywhere ever took Jack Nicklaus or Arnold Palmer to task and asked them to answer for their country's actions.*

Tensions escalated at the 1969 PGA Championship in Dayton, Ohio, when protesters targeted Player. In the third round, Player was paired with Nicklaus, and the group known as the Dayton Organization struck when the golfers were on the tenth green.

According to the Associated Press, Player was jostled and a "heavy, 278-page program was thrown at him on another hole." Further incidents included water thrown on Player and a ball being thrown at him. The protesters approached Nicklaus on the tenth green, too, but he drew back his putter in self-defense. Instead, one of them picked up his ball. Despite it all, Player maintained his composure and wound up finishing second to Raymond Floyd.

By the time Player arrived in Augusta the following spring for the Masters, talk of what had happened in Dayton hadn't cooled off. But the South African tried to downplay it, saying, "It's been exaggerated" when asked about possible protests.

One person who wasn't convinced was Ernest Nipper, Player's longtime Augusta National caddie. Nipper opted to drop Player and work for Chi Chi Rodriguez "for fear that his life was in danger," according to Ward Clayton's account in *Men on the Bag*.

Carl Jackson was assigned to Player, and with tight security surrounding them all week, nothing happened. Player bogeyed the final hole Sunday and missed out on the Billy Casper–Gene Littler playoff by one shot.

While there were serious rumblings about the lack of black golfers at the Masters—no black player was invited or qualified until 1975—Player took a bold step in his home country. "When John Vorster was prime minister, he [Player] went to his residence and said, 'Mr. Vorster I would really like to bring Lee Elder from America to be the first black golfer to play in the South African [PGA],' and he agreed," Vivienne Player said. "Lee Elder, very bravely, came. Which was really the breakdown of apartheid in sport. He did a good job on that."

Elder did compete in the South African PGA in 1971, and it marked the country's first integrated tournament. Elder competed in several other events while in Africa, and he won the Nigerian Open that year. Four years later, Elder made history when he became the first black golfer to compete at the Masters.

Gary Player hits from the bunker as caddie Carl Jackson looks on during the 1970 Masters. Player just missed out on a playoff between Billy Casper and Gene Littler. *Courtesy of the Augusta Chronicle.*

"We felt bad for the black guys. It was hard for them over here, the trouble they had on the tour," Vivienne said. "So it was nice that he could help, and Lee did a great job in South Africa. He played all over. It all worked out very well."

Apartheid came to an end in South Africa in 1994. Mandela was released from prison in 1990, and he began negotiations with President F.W. de Klerk. The country's first multiracial elections were held in April 1994, and the African National Congress won the majority of the vote. Mandela, as the leader of the group, became South Africa's first black president.

In the 2000 British Open, played at St. Andrews, Player donned the same black-and-white pants that he had worn forty years prior to draw attention to his country's plight. This time, he wore them to celebrate the end of apartheid.

Chapter 8

# Coming Back with a Vengeance

Gary Player's devotion to fitness was well established by the early 1970s. He had been exercising for nearly three decades at this point in his life, and the physical training had served him well: he had already claimed a career Grand Slam and was still one of the leading players in the world.

Player added his sixth career major, the 1972 PGA Championship at Oakland Hills, but he planned to undergo surgery at the end of the year. A large cyst had developed behind his left knee, and Player knew he had to take care of it. The operation didn't occur until early February 1973, though, and then another complication set in. Doctors discovered a blockage between his kidney and his bladder, and he underwent his second major surgery.

After sixteen consecutive starts at Augusta National, Player was forced to sit out the Masters. It was rare for a top player to miss a major and something that never happened to Arnold Palmer or Jack Nicklaus during their primes.

Player did return not long after the Masters, which was won by Georgia native Tommy Aaron. Player contended at the U.S. Open, but his only win on the PGA Tour came at the Southern Open. He finished sixty-third on the tour's money list, nowhere near his usual spot among the leaders.

"I had no strength at all," Player told the *Augusta Chronicle*'s Robert Eubanks before the 1974 Masters. "I started to play weeks too soon. It took me about seven months to overcome it. I was in the hospital 40 days and never touched a golf club. But I always was optimistic I would get my game back."

When Masters week arrived, the annual golf tournament in Augusta wasn't even the biggest sports story in Georgia. Hank Aaron's pursuit of

Gary Player admires the Wanamaker Trophy that he won at the 1972 PGA Championship at Oakland Hills in suburban Detroit. *Courtesy of Black Knight International Archives.*

baseball's all-time home run record was dominating headlines, and the Atlanta Braves slugger broke his deadlock with Babe Ruth on Monday, April 8, when he drilled his 715th homer in Atlanta.

Player was determined to make up for lost time and show that 1973 was an aberration by his lofty standards. He played in three PGA Tour events leading into the Masters, and his best showing was a tie for eleventh at New Orleans.

"Yes, I'm hitting it quite nicely," Player said after completing a practice round at Augusta National with Arnold Palmer, Raymond Floyd and Lanny Wadkins. "But you have to do all kinds of things well to win this tournament."

Player's opening two rounds at the Masters were steady but unspectacular. A pair of one-under seventy-ones left Player five shots behind thirty-six-hole leader Dave Stockton. He knew he needed something special as "moving day," the third round, loomed on Saturday.

But nothing Player did in the first nine holes could make up ground on Stockton. While Player made only one birdie and made the turn in one-under thirty-five, Stockton added to his lead. He holed out his third shot for an eagle at the par-five second and followed with a birdie at the short third.

Player's putter warmed up on the second nine, though. He hit a seven-iron to tap-in range at the dangerous twelfth, and then he holed birdie putts of fifteen feet and six feet on the next two holes. He added birdies at Nos. 15 and 16 and made no bogeys en route to six-under sixty-six.

Stockton stumbled on the inward nine with two bogeys and just one birdie, but his seventy was good for a one-stroke lead over Player heading into the final eighteen.

Player credited the low score to a change in his swing that eliminated big hooks from popping up at inopportune times. Player recounted a story in which he sought advice the previous year from Ben Hogan, who suffered from a bad case of the hooks early in his career. While playing in Brazil, he called the golf legend and said this is how their conversation went:

> I said, "Next to you, I've worked so hard, been as dedicated as anyone in golf. And I would like to ask a question about the swing if you will."
> He asked, "Who do you work for on the tour?" And I said, "Dunlop."
> He said, "Well, call Mr. Dunlop!" Pow! Down went the phone.

Player said his advice to anyone seeking advice from the reclusive Hogan would be this: "I'm going to tell all young people who call to say, 'Mr. Hogan, those Hogan clubs are really super.'"

Player's jovial mood continued as he joked that he needed to win out of necessity.

"I have to," he said. "I have my whole family with me and need the money to meet expenses."

Player would have to overtake Stockton and do battle with a number of other challengers. Jim Colbert was tied with Player for second, and another shot back were Phil Rodgers and Bobby Nichols. Jack Nicklaus, always dangerous at Augusta, was five shots behind Stockton entering the final round.

Player applied the early pressure with a birdie at No. 6. The crucial swing came at the par-four ninth, where Player made birdie and Stockton, considered one of the game's best putters, three-putted for a bogey.

But Player's lead was short-lived. He made bogeys at Nos. 10 and 12 but bounced back with a birdie at the thirteenth by holing a six-footer.

Gary Player is congratulated by his caddie, Eddie McCoy, after winning the 1974 Masters. *Courtesy of the* Augusta Chronicle.

As expected, Nicklaus made a charge. An eagle at the par-five thirteenth put him into contention, but bogeys on the final nine holes derailed his effort. Tom Weiskopf hit into the water at the sixteenth to end his chances.

That left the battle to Player and Stockton, and the South African was one up when he reached the seventeenth hole. A fine drive left Player 140 yards from the pin, but Player couldn't help but think about all the trouble the par-four had caused him through the years.

"Eddie, in all the years I've played here, I don't think I've hit this green six times," Player told his caddie, Eddie McCoy.

The two men conferred on club selection, and Player took the nine-iron. The shot not only found the green but also wound up inches from the cup.

"After I hit it I kind of pushed it on the bag and I told my caddie I'm not going to need a putter," Player said. "And there it was, six inches from the hole."

Tommy Aaron (right) helps Gary Player into his green jacket after the South African won his second Masters in 1974. Looking on is Masters chairman Clifford Roberts. *Courtesy of Black Knight International Archives.*

Player tapped in the birdie and then made par at the final hole to secure his two-shot win over Stockton and Weiskopf. A year after sitting out his favorite event of the year, Player was slipping into another green jacket.

At thirty-eight, Player added a second Masters title to his major total and set a record for most years between victories (thirteen). Of even greater importance to the devout Player was that the win came on Easter Sunday. Player's faith, including in his golf game, never wavered. Major surgeries were just minor bumps on his road to victory.

A motto given to Player by evangelist Billy Graham was on his scorecard in the final round. "It said, 'Remember I can do anything in Jesus Christ who strengtheneth me,'" Player said.

# HALL OF FAME

The year 1974 was a big one for Gary Player. Not only did he win two majors, the Masters and the British Open, but he also was inducted into the World Golf Hall of Fame in Pinehurst, North Carolina.

Player was part of the original class of the now-defunct hall that bordered the famed Pinehurst No. 2 course. Joining Player in the inaugural class were Patty Berg, Walter Hagen, Ben Hogan, Bobby Jones, Byron Nelson, Jack Nicklaus, Francis Ouimet, Arnold Palmer, Gene Sarazen, Sam Snead, Harry Vardon and Babe Zaharias.

The World Golf Hall of Fame opened in its present location in 1998 in St. Augustine, Florida. Player is now the global ambassador for the organization and frequently appears in television commercials to promote the facility.

His hall of fame biography contains the following tribute:

> Player is indisputably the greatest international golfer of all time. He estimates he has spent more than three years of his life in airplanes and traveled some 14 million miles. In every year from 1955 to 1982, Player won at least one sanctioned international tournament. He won the World Match Play title five times, the Australian Open seven times and the South African Open 13 times. In winning the 1974 Brazilian Open, he shot the only 59 ever in a national open.

Chapter 9

# Age Is Just a Number

B y 1978, Gary Player was forty-two years old, and his career was beginning to slow down. While he was still capable of winning, particularly tournaments in his native South Africa, Player had not won on the PGA Tour since 1974.

He arrived at Augusta National Golf Club that spring with a new putting stroke and confidence in his game. While American stars Jack Nicklaus, Tom Watson and Raymond Floyd were considered the favorites, no one was giving Player much of a chance. But the South African had taken three months off to rest and spend time with his family, and he came to the year's first major feeling refreshed and relaxed.

Player's new putting stroke—more of a longer effort than his normal jab—had not produced the desired results at the previous week's Greater Greensboro Open. Player finished five shots behind the winner, a young Spaniard named Seve Ballesteros, but that is not what upset him. A newspaper article in Greensboro said that Player was "a fading star."

Player wanted to prove that he was not washed up, but his first two rounds at the Masters did little to convince otherwise. A pair of even-par seventy-twos left Player comfortably within the cut line but put him five shots behind thirty-six-hole leaders Rod Funseth and Lee Trevino.

Augusta National's normally slick Bermuda greens were not as fast as they had been in previous Masters—Nicklaus described them as being "membership speed"—and that befuddled a lot of the veteran players

Gary Player and his caddie line up a shot during the 1977 Masters. *Courtesy of the* Augusta Chronicle.

who had come to know the breaks by memory. Player managed to hole a few putts in the third round, but his three-under-par sixty-nine paled in comparison to Hubert Green's fine sixty-five. At ten under, Green was seven shots clear of Player.

While everyone was anticipating a normal Masters shootout in Sunday's final round, the only person who believed Player had a chance was Player. At dinner Saturday evening, Player's agent, Mark McCormack, announced that he was leaving early Sunday morning since he didn't have any players in the mix. That didn't sit too well with a certain South African golfer, according to oldest son Marc Player.

> *My dad said, "What do you mean you're leaving?" [McCormack] said, "I don't have any of my players in contention. I'm going to go home, see my family and watch the ending on television." And my dad said, "Mark, I can win. I'm only seven back." "Come on Gary, you're seven back. You can't win the Masters." And Dad said, "I think you're wrong. I'm very disappointed in you."*
>
> *Mark was always very analytical. "You have to shoot sixty-four or sixty-five to win tomorrow. No one's ever shot sixty-four or sixty-five in the last round to win at Augusta. What are the chances of that?" Dad said, "The way I'm playing, I hole a few putts, I could easily shoot sixty-four." He said, "Well, OK, my plane's booked, goodbye." And he left. We sat around the table, and my brother Wayne said, "Dad, you're 100 percent right. If you hole a couple of putts you could easily win."*

Player got off to a fast start in the final round with birdies on Nos. 2 and 3, the latter when a thirty-foot putt dropped. He gave back a stroke with a bogey at No. 7, but he got it back after hitting his approach to twelve feet and sinking the birdie putt at No. 9. With nine holes to go, Player still trailed Green by four shots. Watson and Funseth also were ahead of Player.

The veteran South African was paired with Ballesteros, the young man who had won the week before at Greensboro, and the Spaniard was celebrating his twenty-first birthday that Sunday. The two weren't a marquee pairing at the start of the day, but the Masters gallery serenaded Ballesteros with "Happy Birthday" as he walked from the fifteenth green to the sixteenth tee.

"Somewhere in the round a couple of chaps said it's Player, and they didn't know who Ballesteros even was," Marc Player said. "They said let's go, he's got no chance. And my dad heard that and he said, 'Hey, where are you going? Don't leave man, I'm right in it.' And Seve said, 'Gary, you really think you can win it?' And he said, 'Si, Seve, what do you mean? I'm only four back.'"

Player was determined to prove that he could still win.

"He walked over and said, 'Seve, let me tell you one thing,'" Ballesteros recalled in a 2001 television interview. "'These people think I can't win anymore, but today I'm going to show everyone I can still win.'"

Ballesteros didn't know it, but he was about to get the education of a lifetime as the two golfers went to Augusta National's final nine holes.

Player birdied the tenth hole with a twenty-five-foot putt and nearly picked up another birdie when his chip at the eleventh grazed the cup. At the twelfth, a dangerous par-three over Rae's Creek, Player knocked his tee shot to fifteen feet and made that for another birdie.

Now it was time to attack the par-five holes, and Player did just that. At the thirteenth, his four-iron second shot settled some fifteen feet from the cup, and his eagle putt touched the cup before stopping in easy birdie range. After a par at the fourteenth, Player knocked a three-wood shot onto the green at the fifteenth and two-putted for a birdie.

Gary Player receives kisses from daughter Jennifer and son Wayne following his come-from-behind win at the 1978 Masters. *Courtesy of the* Augusta Chronicle.

Now at nine under for the tournament, Player was finally in contention. Green, Watson and Funseth all were going back and forth between nine and ten under, but they had more holes to play. Player knew he needed more birdies if he was going to slip into his third green coat.

At the sixteenth, Player's tee shot left him a ticklish fifteen-footer for birdie. The putt was similar to one he had faced in the final round in 1962. Then, after watching Arnold Palmer hole an impossible chip shot for birdie, Player missed his putt and then lost an eighteen-hole playoff to Palmer.

Not this time.

"The last time I hit it on the right edge of the hole and it didn't break," Player said. "This time I hit it straight in."

Player made par at the seventeenth and came to the final hole in a dogfight for the lead. His approach shot to the eighteenth green settled some fifteen feet away from the front left pin position. Again, Player drew on his memory. In 1970, he had faced a putt on the same line after hitting into the bunker and needing to save par to join a playoff with Billy Casper and Gene Littler. He played too much break and missed it. This time, Player studied the putt from all angles as an excited Ballesteros observed.

Player trusted his new putting stroke, and the ball headed for the cup. As it rattled into the hole, Player clenched his fist and punched the Georgia air. The forty-two-year-old South African had made seven birdies in the final ten holes for a closing sixty-four, which matched the lowest score in Masters history.

His caddie, Eddie McCoy, was excited for personal reasons. Player told *Golf Digest* in 2002:

> *When I arrived there in 1978, Eddie was upset. "You got to win this tournament, man. I'm in trouble, and I need a new house." I don't know what kind of trouble Eddie was in, but when I [shot sixty-four] on Sunday, you've never seen a man as happy as Eddie was. There's a picture taken just after I holed a 15-footer on 18. In it, you see Eddie flying toward me like Batman, with an expression on his face as though he'd just won the lottery.*

While Player, his caddie and his family were certainly thrilled, it wasn't over yet. As he did in 1961, Player had to wait and watch as the final few groups finished up. Augusta National had adopted a new sudden-death playoff format to settle ties, and Player didn't want that at all. Not with a 2-11 playoff record on the PGA Tour and 17 losses overall in playoffs for his career. "It was agony, sheer agony," Player said.

Tom Watson (left) helps Gary Player into his green jacket after Player won the 1978 Masters. Player shot a final-round sixty-four to win at age forty-two. *Courtesy of the* Augusta Chronicle.

Watson joined Player at eleven under with a birdie at the sixteenth, but he was eliminated with his bogey at the final hole when he wound up left of the green and couldn't save par.

That left Green and Funseth as the only men who could catch Player. Funseth had a putt similar to the one Player had made at the eighteenth but barely missed it.

Green had hit his approach to three feet, and it seemed inevitable that he would make it and force the first sudden-death playoff in Masters history. But Green had to back off the putt when he heard radio announcer Jim Kelly calling the action in the greenside booth. When Green did hit the putt, the ball broke across the right lip and missed.

Gary Player—a "fading star," according to some—had become the oldest Masters champion. And he had done it in spectacular style, a sixty-four that was the lowest final round in Masters history.

"The first thing he did was call Mark McCormack," Marc Player said. "'You son of a bitch, see I told you! You should have stayed.' I remember that happening. That's the type of attitude that personifies him so much: 'I can shoot sixty-four, and I will shoot sixty-four.' Mark motivated him to say I'll show you."

The experience was not lost on Ballesteros, either.

"If you watch on the film and that last putt, Seve comes over and he's almost as excited as my dad," Marc Player said. "People call it the Tiger salute, but Gary Player was doing it in 1978. Fist pump. Seve comes over and almost picks him up. And then after he said, 'Gary, Gary, you teach me how to win Masters.'"

## Chapter 10

# Rise of Europe

In the fall of 2011, Gary Player sat back and marveled at the success of international golfers. Young American Keegan Bradley had recently won the PGA Championship to break a streak of six majors in a row won by golfers from outside the United States.

"That is good for golf," Player said. "I'm not American or European, but I look at golf and say this is good for golf. It helps the manufacturers, and it gets golf boosted in their countries. It's a big boost for the game."

For the first time since 1994, all four majors were held by non-Americans. "Isn't that amazing?" he said. "I would have given a thousand to one odds."

Player knows how special the run of international success is. Northern Ireland's Graeme McDowell's win at the 2010 U.S. Open was followed by South African Louis Oosthuizen's victory at the British Open. Germany's Martin Kaymer then won the PGA Championship to end 2010, and South Africa's Charl Schwartzel slipped into the green jacket in 2011. The run was capped by two more wins from Northern Ireland golfers: Rory McIlroy at the U.S. Open and Darren Clarke at the British Open.

In the 1960s and 1970s, Player's glory years, the majors were dominated by Americans. Often, it was Player versus the world: in the 1960s, he won four of the nine majors claimed by non-Americans. In the 1970s, he took four of the seven major trophies that didn't go to the United States. "America dominated for so long. There was no real competition," Player said. "And competition is an essential ingredient to popularize it."

Although Player won the Masters three times during the 1960s and 1970s, he remained the only foreign-born winner at Augusta National. Outside of Harry Cooper's close calls in the early years, the only international player to really challenge at Augusta besides Player was Roberto de Vicenzo. The Argentinian's scorecard gaffe in 1968 robbed him of a chance to meet Bob Goalby in an eighteen-hole playoff.

Although it took nearly twenty years after Player's first win at Augusta, a worthy international player did emerge. It was Seve Ballesteros, and he had grown up learning to play the game by hitting rocks on the coast of Spain. As he grew older, he dreamed of one thing: to win the Masters. "When I was a kid or hitting balls, chipping or putting, I would say this is to win the Masters," Ballesteros said in a television interview.

The charismatic young golfer from Spain quickly made his mark after turning professional when he was sixteen. Ballesteros finished as runner-up at the 1976 British Open, and that earned him his first invitation to the Masters the following spring. He really wasn't a factor in his first three trips to Augusta, but he won the crowd over with his smile and style of play.

The Spaniard won his first PGA Tour event at Greensboro in 1978, and he broke through for his first major championship at the British Open in 1979. Ballesteros was famous for hitting wayward shots with his driver—he famously had to play out of a car park en route to that British Open win—but that only endeared him to his fans even more.

When the 1980 Masters arrived, Ballesteros was a player who could not be overlooked. He quickly put a stranglehold on the tournament with an opening sixty-six that tied him for the lead, and he followed with rounds of sixty-nine and sixty-eight to open up a seven-shot lead.

With such a large lead, a Ballesteros win was deemed a mere formality by the press, who turned their attention to records for margin of victory and seventy-two-hole total that were in his reach. Those records moved closer to reality as Ballesteros again blitzed the front nine, making birdie on three of his first five holes. He made the turn in thirty-three, moving him to sixteen under par for the tournament and ten shots ahead of his closest pursuer.

And then it all began to fall apart.

A three-putt bogey on No. 10 was the first blow, and then a ball in the water at No. 12 produced a double bogey. On No. 13, he dumped his second shot into the water guarding the green and suffered another bogey. Just like that, his ten-shot lead was down to just two over hard-charging Gibby Gilbert, who was playing several holes ahead of Ballesteros.

Seve Ballesteros watches a putt during the 1980 Masters. He became the youngest champion at age twenty-three, a record since broken by Tiger Woods. *Courtesy of the Augusta Chronicle.*

"I was comfortable…10 shots is a lot," Ballesteros said later. "Then I was uncomfortable. I'm in trouble. I was thinking I was about to lose the tournament."

The Spaniard gathered himself to make par on the fourteenth and then hit what he described as the shot of the day on the par-five fifteenth to set

Spain's Seve Ballesteros hugs his caddie after winning the 1983 Masters. Ballesteros was just the second foreign-born player to win the Masters. *Courtesy of the* Augusta Chronicle.

up a two-putt birdie. He parred in from there and won the Masters by four shots over Gilbert and Jack Newton.

The opportunities to break hallowed scoring records had slipped by him. But Ballesteros was most grateful to slip into the green jacket as darkness crept over Augusta National.

"I say I must try hard and, finally, I started playing well,'" Ballesteros said of his back-nine troubles. "I am very pleased."

After the win, Ballesteros wasted little time in praising Player. "I will never forget the way he won the 1978 Masters for the third time. I will never forget that because he tried very hard and he played great," Ballesteros said. "I was even more excited than he on the last hole, I tell you."

Ballesteros added a second green jacket in 1983. Although the tournament finished on Monday because of heavy rains earlier in the tournament, Ballesteros put any suspense to rest early. He played his first four holes in birdie, eagle, par, birdie to open a commanding lead, and he enjoyed a Sunday-like stroll to victory.

Ballesteros was just the tip of the international iceberg that was about to hit golf. A new generation of European players was on the horizon, and they included Englishman Nick Faldo, Germany's Bernhard Langer, Scotland's Sandy Lyle and young Spaniard Jose Maria Olazabal.

Langer joined Player and Ballesteros as international winners at the Masters, and he was soon joined by Lyle and Faldo. The internationals could have really dominated the decade if not for Jack Nicklaus's heroic charge in 1986 and Larry Mize's miraculous chip-in in 1987.

In the 1990s, Europeans continued to excel at the Masters. Ian Woosnam of Wales and Olazabal added victories, while Faldo won two more green jackets and Langer added one as well. For the first time since Bobby Jones and Clifford Roberts started the Masters, more foreign-born players had won in a single decade than Americans.

To this day, European golfers credit Ballesteros for knocking down the barrier and showing them it was possible to win in the United States, including Augusta. Like Player a generation before him, he enjoyed showing the way for others. "As the first European to win the Masters, I think it brought some confidence and inspiration," Ballesteros said in a television interview. "I felt their victories were thanks to me. I feel very proud of that."

Chapter 11

# South African Success

G ary Player's exploits around the globe were lost on a lot of his fellow
South Africans. Television sets were not a household commodity until
the 1970s, and the Internet was decades away from being developed.

"In the 1960s and 1970s we weren't as connected as we are today. South
Africa only got television in 1974," Marc Player said. "It was one channel,
and they weren't showing the Masters. A lot of the baby boom generation of
South Africa never grew up watching him on television."

No South African had followed in Player's footsteps as a major champion,
but one was waiting in the wings. Ernie Els was eight years old when Player
stormed to victory at Augusta National for his final major championship on
the regular tour.

"I remember staying up late with my dad to watch Gary win the 1978
Masters, his third green jacket," Els said. "I was eight years old and had
just started playing golf. I'll never forget how I felt when I saw him make
that putt on the eighteenth green to shoot thirty on the back nine for a final
round of sixty-four. Then Seve giving him a bear hug!"

Els was proficient in soccer, rugby and cricket, and he excelled in tennis.
But the golf bug bit him hard when he saw Player's win. "It made me want
to be exactly like Gary, to follow in his footsteps and be a great champion, a
major winner," Els said. "It was moments like that, which made Gary a hero
in the eyes of a lot of youngsters growing up in South Africa, me included."

Els joined his hero as a major champion when he won a three-man playoff
at the 1994 U.S. Open. Since then, Retief Goosen, Trevor Immelman,

South Africa's Ernie Els hits from the tributary of Rae's Creek on the thirteenth hole at Augusta National Golf Club. Els has twice finished as runner-up at the Masters. *Courtesy of the* Augusta Chronicle.

Louis Oosthuizen and Charl Scwartzel have all added to South Africa's major total. In fact, South Africa's total of twenty-one majors since World War II is second only to the United States.

"That's incredible," Player said. "South Africa has a great climate and great golf courses."

Player has been the patriarch of South Africa golf for more than five decades, but he wasn't the country's first major champion. That distinction fell to Bobby Locke, a putting genius who won four British Opens in a span of less than ten years.

"If you speak to a young guy about Bobby Locke, they don't know too much," Player said. "But he was the best putter the world ever saw. He came over here and won seven out of eleven tournaments. He was so good that they barred him."

Player was referring to the PGA of America's decision to ban Locke. According to Locke's World Golf Hall of Fame biography, the ruling came after the South African won his first British Open in 1949 and elected to stay overseas to play exhibitions rather than come back to the United States and play in tournaments he had committed to. Although the ban was lifted, Locke decided to play most of his golf abroad, and he never won a major outside of the British Open. That left it to Player, Harold Henning, Bobby Cole and other South Africans to take up where Locke had left off.

According to peers like Simon Hobday and Dale Hayes, Player was too focused and too good to beat. He was the epitome of success in his home country, and everyone wanted to knock him off the pedestal. "I played against him three hundred times and beat him once," Hobday said. "Gary had us a two-shot penalty. Every time you played him, you tried so hard to beat him that we all played shit. It was the same thing with Nicklaus and Tiger when they were in their prime. They had a two-shot penalty on everybody else."

Hayes, now a television commentator in South Africa, agreed. "We obviously tried to emulate him and tried to beat him when we turned professional. Of course, he was the bar you had to get to," Hayes said. "He was a very tough competitor. He gave nothing away. It was terrific for South Africans, and I'm sure that's one of the reasons why we've produced so many great golfers is because you had somebody like Gary who set that limit so high."

As Player's career on the regular tours came to a close, there was no real successor from his home country. But he had a pipeline in the works with several promising young players whom he encouraged.

A young man from neighboring Zimbabwe, Nick Price, would be the next big star from Africa. He first made a splash at the 1982 British Open but

Ernie Els blasts out of a bunker at the Masters. Els is a three-time major championship winner, and he said he patterned his career as an international golfer by following Gary Player's example. *Courtesy of the* Augusta Chronicle.

couldn't hold the lead, and Tom Watson swooped in to win the major. Price would make even more noise a few years later at the 1986 Masters. After barely making the cut, Price blitzed the Augusta National layout with ten birdies and just one bogey for a record score of sixty-three. That put him in the final pairing with Greg Norman, but Jack Nicklaus came from behind with a final-round sixty-five that gave him an improbable win at age forty-six. Price learned from his mistakes and continued to improve. In the early 1990s, he rose to No. 1 in the World Golf Rankings and won three majors. The first came at the 1992 PGA Championship. He then followed with victories in 1994 at the British Open and the PGA as non-Americans swept the majors for the first time since the Masters began in 1934.

One of those non-Americans turned out to be a Player protégé. Els beat Loren Roberts and Colin Montgomerie at the U.S. Open in 1994 for his first major. He would become a fixture at the majors, regularly challenging the world's best. Els added a second U.S. Open in 1997 at Congressional Country Club and a British Open in 2002.

Els wasn't the only South African who was a force at the U.S. Open. Retief Goosen won that event twice, in 2001 and 2004, to add to South Africa's résumé. Goosen said he patterned his game after one of the game's all-time greats. But it wasn't Player.

"Well, Gary was a little bit before my time, so he wasn't really someone I looked up to as a junior," Goosen said. "It was more Seve [Ballesteros] and Jack Nicklaus. I mean Jack Nicklaus was one of the guys I patterned my golf after and his books. But Gary became more of a role model for me later in my life, especially the last ten years I've become good friends with Gary. I do a lot of his charity events, so I try to support him, and he's a great person to be around."

Chapter 12

# Senior Grand Slam

A victory in the 1978 Masters seemed to be the perfect sendoff for Gary Player. It was exciting, provided a dramatic finish and was an exclamation point at the end of his remarkable career. The only problem with that theory was that Player wasn't done winning. Not by a long shot.

In his very next start after the improbable Masters win, Player found lightning in a bottle for the second week in a row. He overcame a seven-shot deficit to win the Tournament of Champions. The victim that time, of all people, was Seve Ballesteros. The young Spaniard stumbled to seventy-nine in the final round at La Costa Country Club, and that opened the door for Player to steal the title with his closing sixty-seven.

"I was lucky the wind was up," Player said of the conditions. "You have a much better chance to make up a lot of strokes if the weather is bad."

Player traveled to Houston the following week, looking to make it three in a row. Winning back to back was rare enough, but three in a row was almost unheard of in pro golf. Only Johnny Miller and Hubert Green had done it in recent years.

The South African, though, was never short on confidence. He backed it up with a spectacular opening sixty-four in Houston and then followed with sixty-seven. But a third-round seventy left him three shots behind Andy Bean, and the long hitter extended that lead to five early in the final round.

Before the round, according to Player, the leader and challenger crossed paths. "[Bean] came up to me and said, 'You little runt, you're not going to beat me,'" Player said.

Player was undaunted. He kept plugging away, and he birdied two of the last three holes to post sixty-nine. When Bean missed his birdie putt on the final hole and carded seventy-three, Player had won his third consecutive PGA Tour event.

After the round, the Associated Press reported that someone asked Player if he had to be lucky to win three in a row. It was the perfect setup for one of Player's favorite expressions. "Yes," Player said. "And it's amazing, isn't it? The more you practice, the luckier you get."

There's a colorful story about how Player came up with that phrase. Early in his career, Player developed a reputation for being an excellent bunker player. Most consider him to be the best of all time in that category. Player told *Golf Digest*:

> *I was practicing in a bunker down in Texas and this good old boy with a big hat stopped to watch. The first shot he saw me hit went in the hole. He said, "You got 50 bucks if you knock the next one in." I holed the next one. Then he says, "You got $100 if you hole the next one."*

Gary Player blasts out of a bunker during the 1961 Masters. He held off a challenge by Arnold Palmer for a one-shot victory. *Courtesy of the* Augusta Chronicle.

*Above*: Gary Player helps 1975 Masters Tournament winner Jack Nicklaus slip into his green jacket. *Courtesy of the* Augusta Chronicle.

*Below: From left*: Jack Nicklaus, Arnold Palmer and Gary Player—golf's Big Three—pose for a picture before a Masters Club dinner at the Masters Tournament. The three men have won a total of thirteen times at Augusta National Golf Club. *Courtesy of Black Knight International Archives.*

*Above*: Even in his mid-seventies, Gary Player still follows a rigorous exercise plan. That includes sit-ups performed with dumbbells on his chest. *Courtesy of Black Knight International Archives.*

*Below*: Gary Player was the official host at the Saadiyat Beach Classic, a charity golf tournament. *Courtesy of Black Knight International Archives.*

*Above*: Gary Player is joined by Bollywood star and former Miss India Neha Dhupia at the 2011 Gary Player Invitational in South Africa. *Courtesy of Black Knight International Archives.*

*Below*: Gary Player blasts out of a bunker. He is regarded as the finest bunker player in the history of the game. *Courtesy of Black Knight International Archives.*

*Above*: Gary Player goes for a run with his dog at his family farm in South Africa. *Courtesy of Black Knight International Archives.*

*Below*: Gary Player (right) warms up alongside Tiger Woods in a practice bunker at the 2008 Masters. Player and Woods are two of the five golfers to win a career Grand Slam. *Courtesy of the* Augusta Chronicle.

*Above*: A teary Gary Player hugs his wife, Vivienne, after his press conference following the second round at the 2009 Masters. The round marked the end of Player's competitive career at Augusta National. *Courtesy of the* Augusta Chronicle.

*Below*: Gary Player shows off his strength and dexterity by holding two clubs with two fingers. *Courtesy of Black Knight International Archives.*

*Above*: Gary Player kicks up a leg, to the amusement of caddie Dave King, on the twelfth tee during the first round of the 2006 Masters. *Courtesy of the* Augusta Chronicle.

*Below*: Gary Player tees off to officially open Champions Retreat Golf Club in 2005 in Evans, Georgia. The twenty-seven-hole golf course is the only one in the world to feature nines designed by Player, Arnold Palmer and Jack Nicklaus. *Courtesy of the* Augusta Chronicle.

*Left*: Sam Snead (left) and Gary Player share a laugh at the 2001 Masters. Each man won three times at Augusta National in their hall of fame careers. *Courtesy of the* Augusta Chronicle.

*Below*: Gary Player is congratulated by golf dignitaries during the green jacket ceremony following the 1978 Masters. Player's round of sixty-four remains the lowest score by a champion in the final round. *Courtesy of the* Augusta Chronicle.

*Above*: Gary Player helps Fuzzy Zoeller into his green jacket at the 1979 Masters. Zoeller won the tournament's first sudden-death playoff against Tom Watson and Ed Sneed. *Courtesy of the* Augusta Chronicle.

*Below*: Gary Player watches his shot after coming out of a bunker on the seventh green during the 2001 Masters. *Courtesy of the* Augusta Chronicle.

*Left:* Jack Nicklaus (right) puts his arm around Gary Player on the ninth green as they play in the 2001 Masters. *Courtesy of the* Augusta Chronicle.

*Below*: *From left*: Gary Player, Jack Nicklaus and Arnold Palmer walk across the Byron Nelson Bridge after teeing off on the thirteenth hole at the 2001 Masters. *Courtesy of the* Augusta Chronicle.

*Left*: Gary Player reacts to a good tee shot on the twelfth hole during the 2001 Masters. *Courtesy of the* Augusta Chronicle.

*Below*: Gary Player watches a shot from a bunker at the ninth hole during a practice round at the 2007 Masters. *Courtesy of the* Augusta Chronicle.

Gary Player's first shot wasn't so great, but he teed it up again and holed his shot on the ninth hole of the Par-3 Contest at the 2009 Masters. Arnold Palmer (right) shares the moment as Player reacts. *Courtesy of the* Augusta Chronicle.

*Left*: Gary Player looks to the sky after hitting his tee shot in the bunker on the fourth hole during a practice round at the 2004 Masters. *Courtesy of the* Augusta Chronicle.

*Below*: Arnold Palmer (back) looks on as Gary Player reacts to a near hole in one on the ninth hole of the Par-3 Contest at the 2003 Masters. *Courtesy of the* Augusta Chronicle.

*Above*: *From left*: Gary Player, Jack Nicklaus and Arnold Palmer acknowledge the crowd after completing the Par-3 Contest at the 2003 Masters. *Courtesy of the* Augusta Chronicle.

*Left*: Gary Player blasts out of the bunker at the tenth hole in the opening round of the 2002 Masters. *Courtesy of the* Augusta Chronicle.

*Left*: Gary Player acknowledges the gallery after making his par putt at the tenth hole at the 2002 Masters. *Courtesy of the* Augusta Chronicle.

*Below*: Gary Player kneels and offers a prayer of thanks before stepping onto the eighteenth green at the 2009 Masters. *Courtesy of the* Augusta Chronicle.

Seve Ballesteros is all smiles during the early rounds of the 1986 Masters. In Sunday's final round, he faltered, and Jack Nicklaus charged from behind to win. Ballesteros followed Gary Player as the next international champion at the Masters and won the tournament twice in the 1980s. *Courtesy of the* Augusta Chronicle.

*Right*: Gary Player follows a
shot during a round at Augusta
National Golf Club. With fifty-
two appearances, Player holds
the record for most starts at the
Masters. *Courtesy of the* Augusta
Chronicle.

*Below*: Trevor Immelman (left)
and Ernie Els look on as fellow
South African Gary Player tees off
at the 1999 Masters. Immelman
made the cut as an amateur in
his Masters debut. *Courtesy of the*
Augusta Chronicle.

*In it went for three in a row. As he peeled off the bills he said, "Boy, I've never seen anyone so lucky in my life." And I shot back, "Well, the harder I practice, the luckier I get." That's where the quote originated.*

The victory in Houston turned out to be Player's last on the PGA Tour. He continued to win tournaments around the world, but he was not old enough to join the Senior Tour for golfers fifty and over. When he did turn fifty on November 1, 1985, Player wasted little time in winning. In his debut, he claimed the Quadel Senior Classic in Boca Raton, Florida.

As one of only four men to win the career Grand Slam on the regular tour, Player now turned his sights toward a similar goal. He wanted to add a Grand Slam of the Senior Tour majors.

Now known as the Champions Tour, the Senior Tour majors began their current history in 1980. They have shifted through the years to various sites and courses, and the Senior British Open was not recognized as an official event until 2003. But that doesn't stop Player from counting it among his senior majors.

The Tradition was started in 1989 and instantly accorded major championship status. It is the only one of the five majors that Player has never won. But he had completed a sweep of the senior majors available to him by then.

"They have an American Grand Slam on the Senior Tour with tournaments here, but I'm the only man who has won it with the British Open in our majors," Player said in 2009. "So that Grand Slam, I wanted to win that so badly, and it took so long, considering I only had about an eight- to nine-year span."

In 1986, his first full year on the senior circuit, Player won the PGA Seniors Championship. In 1987, he added the Senior Tournament Players Championship and the U.S. Senior Open. That set him up for his finest year on the Senior Tour in 1988. He started with a win in the Senior British Open at Turnberry. Then he followed it with a victory in the PGA Seniors Championship at PGA National. He capped the spectacular year with a playoff victory over Bob Charles at the U.S. Senior Open at Medinah.

Player added two more majors to his résumé in 1990: the Senior British Open and the PGA Seniors Championship. Player would go on to win a handful of Senior Tour events in the next few years, but he was shut out of the majors from 1991 to 1996.

He provided one last hurrah in 1997 at the Senior British Open, which was played at Royal Portrush in Northern Ireland. As it turned out, fellow

Gary Player won the final major of his career at the 1997 Senior British Open at Royal Portrush in Northern Ireland. Player defeated fellow South African John Bland in a sudden-death playoff. *Courtesy of Black Knight International Archives.*

South African John Bland proved to be his biggest obstacle. The two wound up tied after seventy-two holes, but Player made a birdie to win the sudden-death playoff.

The win at Royal Portrush was Player's ninth senior major, which matched his total of nine regular majors. No other golfer can match Player's nine senior majors, nor can anyone lay claim to winning Grand Slams on both the regular and senior tours. Winning majors on the Champions Tour was a natural extension for Player.

"Then I had a new desire. I wanted to be the first man to win the international Grand Slam on the Senior Tour," Player said in 2009. "And I've won more majors on the Senior Tour than anybody and I'm the only one that's won the international Grand Slam; that's with the British Open in it on the Senior Tour, and that gives me as much a kick as doing it on the regular tour. It might not mean as much to you guys, but being a competitor, it meant an awful lot to me."

Chapter 13

# Captain Player

G ary Player had won the Grand Slam on both the regular and senior
tours, tasted victory 165 times and received virtually every honor
golf had to offer. But he had never captained an international team on his
home soil.

That changed in 2003 when the Presidents Cup, pitting the Americans
versus the top international players not from Europe, was held at the Links
at Fancourt in South Africa. Making the event even sweeter was the fact that
old friend and foe Jack Nicklaus was the captain for the U.S. squad. Player
always regarded Nicklaus with high esteem, and he relished the chance to
get the best of him in competition.

The Presidents Cup didn't have the history of the Ryder Cup, the match
play event pitting the United States against Europe. Nor did it have the
tension and pressure of the Ryder Cup, which had escalated in the mid-
1980s when Seve Ballesteros led a European revival.

Both Player and Nicklaus, two of the most respected men in the game,
made it clear they wanted the Presidents Cup to be played with the proper
spirit. Nicklaus had famously conceded a putt to Tony Jacklin in the 1969
Ryder Cup Matches at Royal Birkdale that enabled the Great Britain and
Ireland team to tie the Americans.

"We want to provide a good platform for the game of golf to grow in
the country we're going to and the countries around the world that are
competing in this event. And the representatives to represent themselves well
and make a good showing," Nicklaus said when announcing his wild-card

picks. "Who wins? Obviously Gary wants to win; I want to win. There's no question about that and it's pride for us to win, but it's not the most important thing. The most important thing is to have a great event."

The U.S. team won the first two Presidents Cup events, in 1994 and 1996, and both were played at Robert Trent Jones Golf Club in Virginia. Nicklaus was the captain in 1998 when it ventured to Australia, and the Americans were soundly defeated. The Americans won in 2000, again at Robert Trent Jones.

Player hoped to keep the streak of the home team winning intact. But like Nicklaus, good sportsmanship was his top priority. Player told reporters in a press conference just before the matches:

> *When Jack Nicklaus and I played a friendly round, we played for $10, and we tried to beat the hell out of each other. This has been the most healthy thing that has ever happened in my association with Jack in the past. We love to beat each other. If one loses—and I have always said that Jack Nicklaus was the best loser in golf. Everybody knows he was the best winner, but one of your great football coaches said, show me a good loser and I will show you a non-winner. Well, that's hogwash. Jack Nicklaus has proven this to be absolute nonsense. We both see eye to eye on our teams behaving extremely well—none of the funny things that have taken place in the Ryder Cup.*

Player's international squad was led by South Africans Ernie Els and Retief Goosen, while Tiger Woods and Phil Mickelson were the top Americans.

On the opening day, Player wasn't disappointed, as his squad won three and a half of the six available points. That euphoria was short-lived, however, as the Americans responded to win seven out of ten points on the second day.

On the third day, the international squad swept the Americans in all six matches to take a twelve and a half to nine and a half lead going into the final day. Player's squad would need just five points in the twelve singles matches to win the Presidents Cup.

As expected, the teams' biggest stars would go head-to-head. Els and Woods were matched against each other in the eleventh pairing of the day, while Mickelson and Goosen would go up against each other earlier in the day.

The Americans won five of the first six singles matches to take the lead. Goosen handled Mickelson, two and one, to pull the teams even. With the

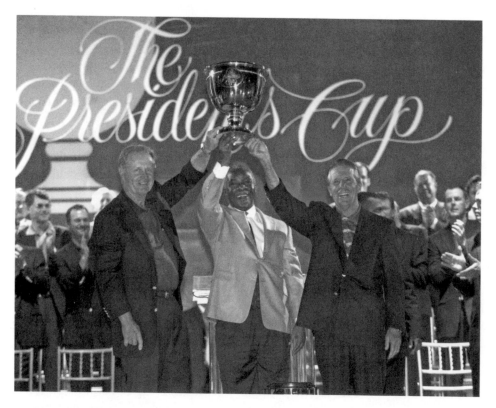

South African president Thabo Mbeki (center) helps Jack Nicklaus and Gary Player hoist the Presidents Cup trophy in 2003. The United States and the International squads battled to a tie and agreed to share the Presidents Cup. *Courtesy of Black Knight International Archives.*

internationals winning two out of the next three matches, the U.S. hopes fell on Woods and Davis Love.

Woods responded with a four and three victory over Els. Love came to the eighteenth hole one up against Robert Allenby but misplayed a chip shot near the green and wound up with a half. After four days of competition, the two teams were tied with seventeen points apiece.

In the case of an overall tie, the rules called for one player from each squad to battle it out in sudden death. Player and Nicklaus each had to submit one name in a sealed envelope before the first day's competition, and it was no surprise that Els and Woods were the men selected.

Woods and Els started the playoff on the eighteenth hole, and both made pars. Next up was the first hole, and again the two men made pars. But now a new problem was creeping up: daylight was quickly running out, and it was clear that only a couple more holes, at best, could be played.

Woods and Els proceeded to the third playoff hole, the par-three second. With enormous pressure on them, both men responded. Woods rolled in a fifteen-foot putt for par, and he pumped his fist like he had just won the Masters. "It was the most nerve-wracking moment I've ever had in golf," Woods said.

Now the pressure shifted to Els. Not only was he playing for his country and his international team, but he also was trying to exorcise some demons against Woods. The young American had gotten the better of Els in several head-to-head showdowns.

Els faced a five-footer for par, and he, too, nailed his putt. But now the question was whether play could continue. In a bizarre scene, Player and Nicklaus and their respective teams gathered to discuss what to do.

The Americans were under the impression that if the matches were declared a tie, they would retain the Presidents Cup. That didn't sit well with the international squad, particularly Els, who wanted to keep on playing.

When Nicklaus offered to call it a tie and share the cup for the next two years, Player and his squad agreed. Even though the competition's official rules called for a winner to be declared, PGA Tour commissioner Tim Finchem agreed to call it a draw.

"I think some people will be upset with that decision. I think some people will probably pan Gary and me for that decision," Nicklaus said. "I think that some people will be unhappy, as they were in 1969. But both Gary and I feel in our hearts, and I think both teams feel that was the right thing to do, and we stand by it."

Chapter 14

# The Businessman

Marc Player's earliest memory of the Masters and Augusta National has nothing to do with his father sinking a putt to win or slipping into a green jacket. The eldest Player son was just a few weeks old when he journeyed to Augusta in time for the 1961 Masters. A few years later, he learned a valuable lesson in rules and respect at Augusta. "I remember running from one place to the other and being tapped on the shoulder by this big burly policeman and he said, 'Son, you're not allowed to run at Augusta National,'" Marc Player recalls with a laugh.

Marc Player is now the chief executive officer of Black Knight International, which oversees the Gary Player Group. Its divisions include golf course design, real estate, business enterprises and the Player Foundation. His focus has turned from being a fan to managing his father's business interests.

"Now I don't really look at it as a son. I look at it as an opportunity," Marc Player said of coming to Augusta. "We rented eight homes last year. We bring in family, friends and business colleagues from all over the world. We have this big Gary Player Group house. It's not party central, but it's certainly headquarters."

Now that he doesn't have a tee time at the Masters, Gary Player is free to do whatever he wants during the first full week in April. But just because he is no longer competing at Augusta National doesn't mean he has slowed down. With family, friends and business associates setting up camp at Champions Retreat not far from the Masters action, Player gets an early start each day. He takes a group out on the nine he designed for a quick round, and then he's back for breakfast and perhaps a workout at the health club. A business meeting with senior executives isn't out of the question. Then he's off to Augusta National, where he can visit the Champions Locker Room in the clubhouse, hold court under the big oak tree outside or just enjoy the action from almost anywhere he pleases.

While some golfers might venture into course design or create their own brand of wine, Player is affiliated with dozens of companies. Some of the best known include Callaway, SAP, Rolex, Coca-Cola and MasterCard. He also is the global ambassador for the World Golf Hall of Fame. With offices in Rio de Janeiro, Cape Town, Johannesburg, Singapore, Shanghai, Abu Dhabi, London and Palm Beach, Florida, Player is still relevant in business circles even more than a decade removed from his last victory.

"I wake up and I think, how do we make Gary Player relevant?" Marc Player said. "How do we keep him relevant? And how do we make the Gary Player brand relevant when he's not around? If we don't, we don't have a business. No one is going to design Marc Player golf courses. No one wants to drink Marc Player wine."

One reason Player remains a force is the way he treats people. "When it comes to entertaining people and having a guest at a golf day, there's nobody who can beat Gary Player," said Dale Hayes, a fellow South African who competed against Player in the 1970s and is now a television commentator. "He remembers people's names, he's got time for everyone, he signs autographs. He's nice to everyone. He's very, very funny. He's got a lovely sense of humor. He listens to people. I don't think there has been, that I know of, many people that were better at doing that job than Gary Player."

Marc Player is full of similar stories about his father. "People love spending time with him. It's contagious," he said. "They'll say, 'He made my day better.' If you're paying him to do this, who's better? I don't know any other. I think three things—value for money, enthusiasm which is contagious and he spreads love wherever he goes."

The chance to entertain clients at the Masters takes on added importance when the host is a three-time winner at Augusta National. Marc said:

*We had a billionaire from Brazil, one of the world's wealthiest men, and he flew up in his new G550. He was about thirty, and this man's got everything. But at the Masters he was like my nine-year-old in Toys R Us. He was so excited. He was running. My dad took him for a sandwich in the Champions Locker Room. I think Tiger said hello. This guy was calling home to say, "I was in the Champions Locker Room with Gary Player. And Tiger stopped to say hi to Mr. Player, and he shook my hand. This is special. What a great place."*

*When he told the story that night, I went wow, for us to have the opportunity to bring our family and friends and business colleagues from India and Brazil and China, the Middle East, from South Africa, to bring them to Augusta for the week, to visit Augusta National and be part of the history of the Masters.*

As a golf course designer, Player has his imprint on courses all over the world. It's no accident that the world's most-traveled athlete has designed courses pretty much anywhere the game is played. Scott Ferrell, president of Gary Player Design, said:

*The fundamental separation is we're willing to get on a plane and go to these emerging markets. He enjoys going into a country that doesn't have*

Gary Player looks over golf course design plans during a site visit. He is dressed in his trademark all-black outfit. *Courtesy of Black Knight International Archives.*

*a lot of golf. We did two projects in Bulgaria, one of them opened about three years ago, the second one opened* [in 2011]. *And that's a country that doesn't have a lot of golf. But he likes to try to help countries and tourism boards bring in people and raise tourism dollars for their country through golf. He's trying to teach young people and get them involved in golf. It's almost like we've mirrored our design company after his playing career. He was one of those guys that would go anywhere and play.*

In late 2011, Player was named one of the finalists to design the course that will be used at the 2016 Olympic Games in Rio de Janeiro. No doubt his proposal was strong on principles that his company has long embraced. Ferrell said:

*There's two cornerstones when it comes down to it: playability, he wants people to enjoy the game, he's not out to design a course for his level, although we do put in championship tees and can make a golf course difficult. He wants a golf course, by and large, to be playable. And he's very concerned with the environment. He really has a personal interest in conserving water, not having too much turf to maintain, he's in tune to the environment. His brother was a world-renowned conservationist, and he had a big influence on him. Environmental, indigenous plant life, saving water, reducing chemicals, he takes all that very seriously. He wants it to be natural. He thinks that's the show.*

# GARY PLAYER'S TEN COMMANDMENTS OF LIFE

1. Change is the price of survival.

2. Everything in business is negotiable except quality.

3. A promise made is a debt incurred.

4. For all we take in life we must pay.

5. Persistence and common sense are more important than intelligence.

6. The fox fears not the man who boasts by night but the man who rises early in the morning.

7. Accept the advice of the man who loves you, though you like it not at present.

8. Trust instinct to the end, though you cannot render any reason.

9. The heights by great men reached and kept were not attained by sudden flight, but that while their companions slept were toiling upward in the night.

10. There is no substitute for personal contact.

Gary Player uses his own set of commandments to guide all aspects of his life. He is fond of all of them, but the ninth one is his personal favorite. "That's what I used to do," Player said. "I used to go to the gym at night and come back after dinner and while my opponents were sleeping. I traveled more, I practiced more. I was toiling up in the night."

And while some athletes might be shy to express their views on religion, Player is not one of them. "I am very, very grateful. I never have a day in my life—a day in my life!—when I don't get on my hands and knees," Player said.

Chapter 15

# Welcome to the Club

In 1985, Gary Player visited the Somerset West course near Cape Town to put on an exhibition. While the golf legend might have been a few years past his prime, he was still one of the most famous people in South Africa. Not surprisingly, a large group of people showed up to get tips and see what Player had to say.

It didn't take long before one of the youngest people in the crowd, a five-year-old boy, worked his way to the front. Before he knew what had hit him, Player had scooped up the young boy and was posing for pictures. You might say Trevor Immelman was destined for a career in golf from that moment forward.

"I was just blown away. He was [almost fifty] then and still pretty damn good," Immelman said. "I'd never seen anything like it, to be honest. I kind of followed him around all day, and he started talking to me. The true man that he is, he just kept in touch with me from then on."

A friendship blossomed that day, and Immelman soon became one of South Africa's leading amateurs.

"Once a year or so, he would send me a note, or see me somewhere, and always encouraged me," Immelman said. "When I was twelve or thirteen, we started playing rounds together. It was a tremendous advantage for me to get some knowledge from him."

Thirteen years after meeting Player for the first time, Immelman won the U.S. Public Links championship and a berth in the Masters. The

Masters winners Trevor Immelman (left) and Gary Player have a laugh on the first tee during a practice round at the 2009 Masters. Immelman joined South Africa's roster of major winners with his victory at the 2008 Masters. *Courtesy of the* Augusta Chronicle.

following April, Immelman shared a practice round at Augusta National with Player and Ernie Els. It is customary for Masters officials to pair amateurs with former champions, and for Immelman they lined up a special treat. He would be paired the first two days with Player, his mentor and boyhood hero.

When he reached the first tee, Immelman said, "Mr. Player, I'm so nervous." The response was swift and reassuring. "Don't worry, Trevor," Player said. "So am I."

Immelman went on to make the cut that year, and before long, he turned professional and won on the South African and European tours. Player selected Immelman for the Presidents Cup team in 2005, and Immelman followed that with his first PGA Tour win at the Western Open. The victory helped him snare PGA Tour Rookie of the Year honors in 2006.

Immelman was plagued the following year by a series of maladies that kept him in and out of hospitals. Just before the 2007 Masters, an intestinal parasite caused him misery, and Immelman dropped more than twenty pounds. Later in the year, on his annual return to South Africa, Immelman won the Nedbank Challenge. But the next week, he noticed a pain in his ribs that caused him to withdraw from the South African Open. Doctors eventually diagnosed it as a fibristic tumor attached to his diaphragm. Biopsy results were negative, and after the health scare, Immelman was cleared to play.

Coming into the 2008 Masters, Immelman was not on anyone's radar screen as a top pick. He had tied for fifth in 2005 thanks to a third-round sixty-five, and he made a hole in one on the sixteenth in the final round. But his other results at Augusta—two finishes in the fifties and two missed cuts—did not make him a favorite.

Enter Player, who was making his record fifty-first appearance that year. Always full of optimism, he turned his words on his young protégé. "I played with him on Tuesday, so we had a practice round," Immelman said. "He was telling me I was playing well, and I was playing well enough

Trevor Immelman (left) and Gary Player played a practice round together at the 2009 Masters. Immelman drew inspiration from Player and joined him as a Masters champion. *Courtesy of the* Augusta Chronicle.

to win." Some putting advice from his brother Mark, the golf coach at Columbus State, also helped.

Immelman took the advice to heart. A first-round sixty-eight gave him a share of the lead with Justin Rose, and another sixty-eight on Friday put him in front of the pack.

Before he teed off Saturday, he received a voicemail from Player. Again, the words of encouragement inspired Immelman, and he shot sixty-nine to take a two-shot lead into the final round.

Player had missed the thirty-six-hole cut and was heading overseas before the Masters would be decided. But he left another voice message for Immelman on Sunday and told his fellow South African that he would have to battle the weather, his own self-doubts and a host of challengers that included world No. 1 Tiger Woods.

As usual, Player was right on all counts. A stiff breeze whipped across Augusta National that Sunday afternoon, with gusts up to thirty miles per hour, and scoring was difficult. Immelman and his young playing partner, Brandt Snedeker, struggled to make birdies.

Immelman kept grinding out pars, however, and by the fifteenth hole had increased his lead to five shots over Snedeker. A final-round charge by Woods didn't materialize, and the South African had enough of a cushion that even a double bogey on the sixteenth hole couldn't hold him back.

Pars on the final two holes gave Immelman a three-shot victory over Woods, and he flexed his muscles on the eighteenth green after tapping in his final putt.

Halfway across the world, as Player's jet landed in Abu Dhabi, the anxious veteran wanted to find out how Immelman had fared. When he found out that another South African would be joining him in the Champions Club, Player beamed with pride as he picked up the phone to call and congratulate him.

"I was very proud of him," Player said. "I said, 'I've been telling you for a long time what a wonderful golfer you are, and I wasn't dreaming.' I think having played fifty-five years as a pro, I could see if he was going to be good or not. And I said, 'Now you've got to start believing in yourself.'"

Looking back, Immelman knows how fortunate he is to have Player in his camp. He said:

*I probably spend more time with him than any of the other guys. I think he kind of saw a little bit of me in him, stature-wise and the way we both work hard and practice hard. I guess he took me under his wing.*

*Also to be fair, at that point when he was kind of finishing up on the Champions Tour, I was still a junior, and Ernie and Retief were kind of established already. For me it was more of a young kid that he could help. It was probably more of the age situation at that point. I was just lucky, in the right place at the right time.*

## Chapter 16
# Calling It Quits

In 1998, at the age of sixty-two, Gary Player made the thirty-six-hole cut at the Masters Tournament with opening rounds of seventy-seven and seventy-two. At the time, he was the oldest golfer to ever make the cut at Augusta National.

But change was on the horizon, and it didn't bode well for senior golfers like Player or his rivals Arnold Palmer and Jack Nicklaus. Technology in golf was allowing players to hit the ball farther than ever, and golf courses were fighting back by making their layouts longer and harder.

Augusta National was no exception. The masterpiece created by Alister MacKenzie and Bobby Jones in the early 1930s had seen plenty of changes through the years, but the course underwent its biggest overhaul in time for the 2002 Masters. Nine holes were altered, and 285 yards were added.

Four years later, Augusta National added another 155 yards and changed six holes. With the course now measuring over 7,400 yards, older players could no longer carry the ball far enough off the tee to clear slopes and gain extra yards of roll. Second shots to par-four holes now required long irons or fairway woods.

Palmer bowed out in 2004 with his fiftieth consecutive Masters appearance, a record. Nicklaus, who had famously challenged for a green jacket as recently as 1998, said his goodbyes in 2005. Older champions like Billy Casper, Charles Coody and Tommy Aaron also bowed out.

Player, though, continued on. As golf's reigning iron man and a champion of physical fitness, he wanted to lead by example and show that a healthy

lifestyle could pay handsome rewards. He also wanted to set the record for most Masters appearances. Palmer held the record with fifty in a row, and that was a mark Player could not touch because he had sat out the 1973 Masters. But getting to fifty-one total was still within his reach.

The chance for doing that took a strange twist before the 2003 Masters. Augusta National and Masters chairman Hootie Johnson, irked at some older players who had a penchant for showing up and withdrawing after just a few holes, announced that former winners who were past age sixty-five or who no longer actively participated in tournament golf would no longer be eligible to play. The policy would take effect in 2004.

The new policy was like a punch to the gut for Player. Johnson was taking away the long-standing privilege that had been extended by Clifford Roberts and Bobby Jones from the very beginning: a Masters champion has a lifetime exemption to compete.

Most former champions abided by the informal gentleman's agreement that they would bow out when the time had come. In 2002, Johnson sent letters to former champions Casper, Gay Brewer and Doug Ford asking them to no longer compete in the tournament. Ford withdrew from his final four Masters appearances, including in 2001, when he quit after one hole.

But Johnson reconsidered his decision a few weeks before the 2003 tournament. At the urging of Palmer and Nicklaus—who were both Augusta National members—he rescinded the rule. Player had told more than one person that he "didn't feel welcome" at Augusta anymore, but he changed the tune when Johnson changed his mind.

"When I stop playing [in the tournament] I will come back, where I wasn't planning to," Player said in 2003. "I was coming there with a feeling of not being all that welcome. Now I come with a great feeling of joy in my heart."

With no obstacles in his path, Player continued to arrive in Augusta each spring and fully participate in Masters Week activities: playing practice rounds, attending the Champions Dinner, competing in the Par-3 Contest and taking on Augusta National once the Masters began.

In 2007, Player competed in his fiftieth Masters to match Palmer for the number of tournaments played. He missed the cut with rounds of eighty-three and seventy-seven, but after the second round, he crowed about his

*Opposite*: Gary Player receives a standing ovation as he crosses the Sarazen Bridge near the fifteenth green at the 2009 Masters. It was Player's record fifty-second appearance as a competitor at the Masters. *Courtesy of the* Augusta Chronicle.

score, as cold and windy conditions prevailed that week. "I played so well it encourages me to come back again," he told reporters. "I want to show people about fitness."

Player surpassed Palmer with his fifty-first appearance in 2008. The South African, though, knew his time was running out. On April 6, 2009, he held a news conference before the Masters started. "I've decided that I would like to make this my last appearance in the tournament," Player told the assembled media that day.

Player shot seventy-eight in the first round and would need a very low score in the second round to make the thirty-six-hole cut. It didn't happen, but Player soaked in the applause at each hole as he made his farewell appearance at Augusta National.

When he got to the eighteenth hole, Player took off his hat to acknowledge the ovation at the green. And then he dropped to one knee to offer a prayer of thanks and show his appreciation. He later said:

> *I'll never forget that as long as I live. It just went on and on and on from all sides. But it happened on every single hole—all thirty-six holes, I got a standing ovation. I wish I had the vocabulary of Winston Churchill to say the correct thing, but it was a feast. It was something you'll never, ever forget. You'll go to your grave knowing you had tremendous love showered upon yourself.*

As he finished off his round of eighty-three and headed off to sign his scorecard, one final treat awaited him. A group of young South Africans competing in the tournament—Trevor Immelman, Richard Sterne, Louis Oosthuizen and Rory Sabbatini—was on hand to greet him. Ernie Els and Retief Goosen were still on the course when Player finished.

Player was touched by the gesture, and he knew that his mission was complete. The future of the game was in good hands. "To have these young guys out there on my last shot of the day, to be there to wait for me to come in, I say, 'Thank you.'"

## Chapter 17

# A Special Anniversary

In 2011, Augusta National celebrated the seventy-fifth playing of the Masters. Its founding fathers, Bobby Jones and Clifford Roberts, had lived to see their event become one of the most important and special in all of sports, and their successors have kept the traditions alive and well.

All week long, there was a sense that something special would occur. Would Tiger Woods break out of his slump and move a bit closer to Jack Nicklaus's record of eighteen professional majors? Would Phil Mickelson defend his title and join exclusive company with his fourth Masters win? Or would one of the game's young stars rise to the occasion?

There was precedent for feeling that a special week was ahead. After all, memorable moments in tournament history happened in the twenty-fifth and fiftieth events. Gary Player became the first international champion in 1961, and Jack Nicklaus roared out of the pack to become the oldest champion in 1986. What would happen in the seventy-fifth?

International golfers once again made up more than half the field, with fifty-three of the ninety-nine participants coming from abroad. The foreign-born players had dominated the majors in 2010, winning the U.S. Open, British Open and PGA. A win at Augusta National would mean that all four majors had been held by players from outside the United States since 1994.

True to form, it didn't take long for the foreign players to put their stamp on the tournament. Thursday's opening round featured excellent scoring conditions, and the players took advantage. Northern Ireland's Rory McIlroy and Spain's Alvaro Quiros shared the lead with sixty-fives, and hot on their heels were a pair of Koreans, K.J. Choi and Y.E. Yang, who shot sixty-sevens. A total of thirteen players made up the top ten and ties, and nine of those players were international stars like South Africans Trevor Immelman and Charl Schwartzel, who each started with sixty-nines.

Friday's second round featured more of the same—that is, a young international player blitzing Augusta National to vault into contention. Australia's Jason Day shot eight-under sixty-four to move into second place behind McIlroy. Day, who was making his Masters debut, proved that experience is not always necessary.

Day and McIlroy were grouped with Rickie Fowler the first two days. All three are budding stars and in their early twenties. The three combined to make thirty-four birdies in the first two rounds. "We fed off each other, and the crowd was behind us," McIlroy said.

Lurking three shots behind McIlroy, though, was Woods. The four-time Masters champ shot sixty-six to leap into contention in a round that featured nine birdies.

Woods's good fortune didn't carry over to Saturday's third round. He struggled to seventy-four and was seven behind McIlroy, who shot two-under seventy to carve out a four-stroke lead going into the final round.

Four international players—Argentina's Angel Cabrera, South Africa's Schwartzel, Australia's Day and Korea's Choi— were tied for second. That meant that no American player was in the top five through fifty-four holes for the first time in Masters history. The leading American was unheralded Bo Van Pelt, who shot sixty-eight to jump into the top ten.

Two birdies late in his round padded McIlroy's lead, and the one at the seventeenth hole came from the back of the green and was punctuated by the youngster's exuberant fist pump as the ball dropped into the cup. With a four-shot lead and eighteen holes to go, some began the coronation process for McIlroy. A win would make him the second youngest Masters champion behind Woods and surely would be the first of many big victories.

Wiser, more experienced players preferred to see how Sunday's action unfolded. That included Player, a man who had won at Augusta both ways: from the front and from way behind.

"Today will be the most important single round of his life, and if he can win today it will enable him to go on and win a lot of major championships," Player said before the leaders teed off Sunday. "But we have a lot of guys, and we have a young man from South Africa, Charl Schwartzel, that I'm also pulling for. We have a fascinating day ahead of us."

Charl Schwartzel holed out twice from off the green in the final round of the 2011 Masters. He chipped in for birdie at the first hole and then holed out for eagle on the third hole as he went on to win. *Courtesy of the* Augusta Chronicle.

Player didn't know how prescient his words would prove to be. It would turn out to be a day unlike any other in Masters history.

Schwartzel made the early noise, chipping in for birdie at the first hole to get off to a hot start. "I don't think I've ever heard a roar that loud around me," he said. "That was a great way to start."

It got better two holes later when Schwartzel holed his second shot for an eagle. His sand wedge from 114 yards hit to the right of the pin and then spun back and trickled into the cup at No. 3. With McIlroy's bogey at the first hole, the four-shot deficit was erased, and the two men were tied for the lead at eleven under.

Schwartzel would drop back with a bogey at the par-three fourth, and he then rattled off ten pars in a row. But all around him, there was plenty of action to be had.

South Africa's Charl Schwartzel acknowledges the gallery on the eighteenth hole in the final round of the 2011 Masters. Schwartzel finished with four birdies to win his first major championship. *Courtesy of the* Augusta Chronicle.

Woods started seven shots behind, but he quickly made up ground with four birdies and an eagle at the par-five eighth to go out in thirty-one.

McIlroy made the turn with a one-shot lead, but that quickly evaporated. His tee shot on the tenth ricocheted way left and wound up between a pair of Augusta National cabins. From there, he pitched out and then hit his third shot left of the green. It took him two more shots to reach the green, and then he two-putted for a devastating triple bogey.

After making bogey at the eleventh, McIlroy unraveled at the par-three twelfth. His tee shot safely found the small green, but he then four-putted for a double bogey. When his tee shot at the thirteenth found the tributary of Rae's Creek, McIlroy slumped over his driver. His chances were gone.

McIlroy's collapse opened the door for a host of challengers. Woods cooled off after his hot start and missed several putts on the final nine, where he could do no better than even-par thirty-six.

Angel Cabrera, the 2009 Masters winner, was paired with McIlroy in the final twosome, but he could not generate a charge on the final nine. The same went for Choi, who made three bogeys on the final nine after flirting with the lead.

With five holes to go, nine players were within two shots of the lead. The main contenders left were a trio of Australians—Geoff Ogilvy, Adam Scott and Jason Day—and Schwartzel, the South African. Ogilvy made five birdies in a row from the twelfth through sixteenth to reach ten under and a share of the lead. Scott overtook him with three birdies, and he finished with a twelve-under total. That was matched by Day, the Masters rookie, who birdied his final hole.

Playing just behind Scott and Day was Schwartzel, and after his hot start, he had churned out par after par. Through fourteen holes he was ten under for the tournament and in the mix. He made his move at the fifteenth, hitting the par-five in two and getting down in two putts for his birdie.

At the sixteenth, his fifteen-foot putt from beneath the hole went in for birdie. At the seventeenth, Schwartzel's drive strayed a bit to the right, but he still hit his approach to twelve feet and made that. Now he held the outright lead.

At the eighteenth, the South African didn't let up. His drive left him 130 yards to the pin, and he chose a "stock, standard wedge." He played it beautifully, and the ball settled eighteen feet right of the cup.

When the putt fell, Schwartzel clenched his fists and celebrated. With birdies on his final four holes, he had done something no one else had ever done—not Nicklaus, not Palmer, not Player —to claim his first major championship.

At Champions Retreat Golf Club, a few miles from Augusta National, Player watched with equal parts awe and pride as Schwartzel mounted his amazing finish. "Four birdies in a row on that golf course is one of the most exciting things I think I ever saw," Player said.

Player had left Augusta National early Sunday afternoon to watch the action with clients and friends. When Schwartzel emerged as the winner, the media clamored for Player's reaction.

"We brought in a lot of people who were going to play the next day," said Scott Ferrell, president of Gary Player Design. "They were at the home and watched the final round with Gary. Not only did they get to see the excitement of seeing a South African win, he then got on the cell phone and did an interview on the Golf Channel. He was on the balcony, and we had it on the TV. People got a charge out of that."

Chapter 18

# Honorary Starter

In nearly sixty years of playing professional golf, Gary Player has had the opportunity to play with people from all walks of life. From the best players to rank amateurs, from celebrities to heads of state, Player has seen it all. In a personal collection of special letters he has received are correspondence from the Dalai Lama, Mother Teresa, Winston Churchill and Nelson Mandela.

Marc Player is the steward of the letters, and in 2011, Player received another special letter. This one was postmarked Augusta, Georgia, and it was from Augusta National and Masters chairman Billy Payne. It was an invitation to become an honorary starter at the Masters and join Arnold Palmer and Jack Nicklaus in the cherished rite of spring.

"For decades, Gary Player has been the international ambassador for the game of golf," Payne said in announcing the honor. "His significant accomplishments at the Masters, spread over an astounding 52 appearances, have helped form many lasting memories for fans of golf around the world. As an honorary starter, his legacy will be rightfully celebrated alongside two of the tournament's other all-time greats, Arnold Palmer and Jack Nicklaus."

Both Palmer and Nicklaus said they were honored to have their fellow Big Three member join them on the first tee at Augusta National.

"It's certainly very appropriate that Gary will be joining Jack and me on the first tee at Augusta next April," Palmer said. "It will be great fun to have the three of us together again kicking off the 2012 Masters at a club and course that meant so much to us and our careers."

Nicklaus concurred:

*From left:* Jack Nicklaus, Gary Player and Arnold Palmer walk to the third green at the Par-3 Contest at the 2011 Masters. *Courtesy of the* Augusta Chronicle.

> *Gary, Arnold and I each have such fond and special memories of our experiences in the Masters, and, collectively, we have many cherished memories of the years we competed together, traveled together, the time our wives and families spent together, the laughs we shared, and the friendship we forged. I would be hard-pressed to name any closer friends in golf and I look forward to the opportunity to reunite once again on the first tee at Augusta National.*

Player couldn't have possibly imagined that he would receive such an honor when he teed off in his first Masters in 1957. "The day we told him, he felt honored," Marc Player said.

In his prepared statement, Player told of his special link to his good friends and golf legends:

> *When I won my first green jacket in 1961, Arnold put it on my back. In 1962, Arnold beat me in an 18-hole playoff to win his second in three years. The year after my second win in 1974, Jack became the* [first

to win five Masters]. *I was there to put the green jacket on both of them. Moments like those are so special and to be able to experience those memories with friends and competitors is something I will never forget.*

According to Marc Player, Payne had worked behind the scenes to get all three men as honorary starters. The tradition began in 1963 with Jock Hutchison and Fred McLeod, and it thrived in the 1980s and 1990s as Gene Sarazen, Byron Nelson and Sam Snead made Thursday morning one of the highlights of the week.

But the tradition was put on hold following 2002 as age took its toll. With Payne twisting some arms, Palmer began hitting the ceremonial shot in 2007, and Nicklaus joined him in 2010. "The chairman had discussed it, going back two years ago when Palmer was doing it on his own, and he got the three of them together and said, 'Look, we're going to phase all three of you into it,'" Marc Player said.

The three men annually play the Par-3 Contest together, but it is rare for the three to appear together on the first tee at the Masters. In 2000 and 2001, the trio played the opening two rounds together.

Palmer and Nicklaus are the only former champions to be invited to become club members; Player has not yet received that invitation. And while other legends have their names affixed to landmarks at Augusta National—Ben Hogan, Byron Nelson and Gene Sarazen all have bridges named for them—Player has no such monument. Palmer and Nicklaus also have plaques affixed to drinking fountains, but Player has not yet been honored in such a manner.

When asked if he feels he should be a club member or honored in a different way, Player demurs and gives a respectful answer. "That's not for me to decide," he said.

Marc Player is more outspoken on the subject:

> *If you look at who has been honored and you look at what he has done, you have to say, "Why not?" Depending on who you are, you'd answer, "I don't have a clue." Others might say he's been outspoken about the right that was granted in perpetuity for a winner to come back and play. And he has expressed views sometimes over the years that perhaps would have been…an American would have said that's not politically correct. A South African or European, we weren't raised to be politically correct. We're raised to be honest, respectful, and my dad has done that by answering honestly.*

*Some would say, "Why hasn't he been made an honorary member?"
Some might say, "Why hasn't he been honored in other ways?" Some might
say, "Why not a water fountain or a bridge?" I think, depending on who's
been chairman and who's been on the committee, how good a friend of the
Masters has Gary Player been? But if you scratch a little beyond those
comments, there is no one past, present—no two golfers, we're not talking
about chairmen or members because that's their obligation—there have not
been two golfers who have done more to promote the Masters.*

*I know de facto how much my father loves, and I don't say love in a light
way, he loves Augusta National. He loves this golf tournament. He tells
everyone all over the world what a fantastic tournament it is.*

Player is looking forward to the reunion of the Big Three. "We traveled
around the world trying to promote golf. We weren't making large sums of
money when we played," Player said. "There was no money. But it was the
challenge of winning. It was a wonderful time. That's why it's so nice for the
three of us to tee off together at Augusta in April because we've grown up
together, been together, competed together and raised money together, so
it's going to be nice."

Bobby Jones once said that if all his life experiences were taken away
except for those at St. Andrews, he still would have lived a rich and full life.
So it is for Player, whose career will come full circle when he serves as an
honorary starter. He'll get a chance to reflect on his three Masters triumphs
and his record fifty-two appearances, and he'll probably remember a few
that got away. He even thinks about Augusta beyond his time on earth.

"If there's a golf course in heaven, I hope it's like Augusta National," Player
is fond of saying. "I just don't want an early tee time."

Chapter 19

# The Future

Playing in the Masters in the 1950s and early 1960s had some added benefits, particularly if you were a golfer of Gary Player's caliber.

Dwight D. Eisenhower was president of the United States from 1953 to 1961, and he also was an Augusta National member. He often visited the club, and he became friends with top golfers like Player and Arnold Palmer. Player had the opportunity to dine with the president one evening, and he never forgot his words of advice.

"I was very honored and privileged to have been around with President Eisenhower when I came here, and Arnold and I had dinner with him and he said something very significant," Player told the media in 2009. "He said, 'America is a very global society.' And how correct he was. He said, 'Base your golf on that,' which I really did. I've played all around the world and made a lot of friends. It's been a great education. Also, it's nice to feel that possibly my wins I experienced here encouraged the international players to realize that they could win."

Five decades later, Player deserves credit for helping popularize a game that now has professional tours all over the globe with golfers competing for hundreds of millions of dollars each year. But it wasn't always like that. Americans, by and large, stayed away from the British Open in the 1930s, 1940s and 1950s because of cost and time constraints.

Palmer also took President Eisenhower's advice to heart and played around the world. He gets credit for bringing Americans back to the British Open because in 1960, after winning the Masters and U.S. Open, he traveled overseas to see if he could win a Grand Slam in a single year. He finished second that year but came back to win the British the following two years.

Like Player and Palmer, Nicklaus wasn't shy about taking his game overseas. "I have always felt golf was a global game. I always was upset with our players when they tried to legislate not allowing the foreign players to come in and play our game here in the United States and made it difficult for them," Nicklaus said in 2010. "I didn't think that was right. We go over there and they said they didn't want them to come here cherry-picking our tournaments. If you can't beat them, then legislate. Get your golf clubs, go practice and beat them."

With international golfers now comprising the majority of the field in the Masters and World Golf Championship events, Nicklaus said that is healthy for the game. "I am proud that I was a part of it, that Arnold was part of it, Gary was part of it. Gary globe-trotted more than any of us," Nicklaus said. "To be able to play outside the United States, around the world, and to be successful around the world and take your game for those people to help grow it in those places."

Player can see that the future is in good hands. The golf world is filled with players like young South African Branden Grace, who won back-to-back European Tour events in January 2012. He was the first player since Fred Couples in 1995 to back up his first European victory with another win.

Grace earned his European Tour card in late 2011, and he won the Joburg Open to get into the winners-only field at the Volvo Golf Champions. The tournament was held at the Links at Fancourt, a Player design that was the site of the 2003 Presidents Cup.

At the Volvo, Grace wound up in a sudden-death playoff with Ernie Els and Retief Goosen. He birdied the first extra hole to claim victory over two of his country's icons. "It's a dream come true to win such a big event—pretty much the best tournament I've played in so far," Grace said.

Player, as he does most every week, was quick to congratulate the winner. Player and his staff often use Twitter and Facebook to stay in touch. He tweeted: "Amazing Grace indeed. Branden Grace won back to back Euro Tour events and beat Goosen & Els in a playoff at Fancourt. Congratulations!"

At the end of 2011, international players were dominating the game in every way imaginable. The top five players in the final World Golf Ranking were non-Americans, and only eighteen of the top fifty players in the world were from the United States. Eight of the top one hundred, in fact, came from South Africa. Throw in the recent domination of the majors by international players, and you can see why Player is always smiling. And while not every young golfer looks to him directly for inspiration, he's still responsible.

Just look at Els and Goosen, who are now carrying the torch. Els said of Goosen:

> *We're the same age and we played a lot of junior golf together when we were growing up, so it's pretty cool that we ended up winning a couple of U.S. Opens each. You have an obligation to the next generation when you play at that level. You get drawn into that position and I like to think that we've conducted ourselves in the correct way throughout our careers and played golf with the right attitude. That's an important lesson for all young golfers to learn.*

Player likes to say that "memories are the cushions of life," and who could blame him if he decided to reduce his schedule and enjoy those memories a little bit more? But that's not Gary Player. After all these years, he is still on a mission to change the world.

"You can't help but admire the man. His strength of mind, dedication and talent made him a winner, a true champion," Els said. "Personally, I think his attitude embodies everything that matters in professional golf. He is a 100 percent legend of the game, an inspiration and a man who I am happy to call a good friend."

Player reasons that if he could overcome a tough childhood in a faraway land and go on to become a champion, others can do it as well.

"I think adversity at the time is a very good thing for you. Everyone has problems," Player said. "And I think the attitude is important. A lot of people say 90 percent is what happens to me and 10 percent is how I react to it. It's 10 percent what happens to you and 90 percent how you react."

Appendix I

# Gary Player's Record at the Masters

| YEAR | SCORES | PLACE | WINNINGS |
|------|--------|-------|----------|
| 1957 | 77-72-75-73—297 | T-24th | $700 |
| 1958 | 74-76—150 | MC | $350 |
| 1959 | 73-75-71-71—290 | T-8th | $1,740 |
| 1960 | 72-71-72-74—289 | T-6th | $2,800 |
| 1961 | 69-68-69-74—280 | WIN | $20,000 |
| 1962 | 67-71-71-71—280 | 2nd | $12,000 |
| 1963 | 71-74-74-70—289 | T-5th | $4,000 |
| 1964 | 69-72-72-73—286 | T-5th | $3,700 |
| 1965 | 65-73-69-73—280 | T-2nd | $10,200 |
| 1966 | 74-77-76-72—299 | T-28th | $1,175 |
| 1967 | 75-69-72-71—287 | T-6th | $4,150 |
| 1968 | 72-67-71-72—282 | T-7th | $3,460 |
| 1969 | 74-70-75-76—295 | T-33rd | $1,425 |
| 1970 | 74-68-68-70—280 | 3rd | $14,000 |
| 1971 | 72-72-71-69—284 | T-6th | $5,600 |

| Year | Scores | Place | Winnings |
|------|--------|-------|----------|
| 1972 | 73-75-72-71—291 | T-10th | $3,600 |
| 1973 | Invited, did not participate | | |
| 1974 | 71-71-66-70—278 | WIN | $35,000 |
| 1975 | 72-74-73-73—292 | T-30th | $1,950 |
| 1976 | 73-73-70-79—295 | T-28th | $1,950 |
| 1977 | 71-70-72-74—287 | T-19th | $2,500 |
| 1978 | 72-72-69-64—277 | WIN | $45,000 |
| 1979 | 71-72-74-71—288 | T-17th | $2,700 |
| 1980 | 71-71-71-70—283 | T-6th | $9,958 |
| 1981 | 73-73-71-71—288 | T-15th | $5,500 |
| 1982 | 74-73-71-74—292 | T-15th | $5,850 |
| 1983 | 73-78—151 | MC | $1,610 |
| 1984 | 71-72-73-71—287 | T-21st | $6,475 |
| 1985 | 71-75-73-75—294 | T-36th | $3,612 |
| 1986 | 77-73—150 | MC | $1,500 |
| 1987 | 75-75-71-76—297 | T-35th | $4,257 |
| 1988 | 78-75—153 | MC | $1,500 |
| 1989 | 76-77—153 | MC | $1,500 |
| 1990 | 73-74-68-76—291 | T-24th | $11,000 |
| 1991 | 72-75—147 | MC | $1,500 |
| 1992 | 75-73—148 | MC | $1,500 |
| 1993 | 71-76-75-80—302 | 60th | $3,700 |
| 1994 | 71-79—150 | MC | $1,500 |
| 1995 | 76-73—149 | MC | $1,500 |
| 1996 | 73-76—149 | MC | $1,500 |
| 1997 | 76-75—151 | MC | $5,000 |
| 1998 | 77-72-78-75—302 | 46th | $11,200 |
| 1999 | 79-79—158 | MC | $5,000 |
| 2000 | 76-74—150 | MC | $5,000 |

| Year | Scores | Place | Winnings |
|------|--------|-------|----------|
| 2001 | 73-76—149 | MC | $5,000 |
| 2002 | 80-78—158 | MC | $5,000 |
| 2003 | 82-80—162 | MC | $5,000 |
| 2004 | 82-80—162 | MC | $5,000 |
| 2005 | 88-79—167 | MC | $5,000 |
| 2006 | 79-81—160 | MC | $5,000 |
| 2007 | 83-77—160 | MC | $10,000 |
| 2008 | 83-78—161 | MC | $10,000 |
| 2009 | 78-83—161 | MC | $10,000 |

Source: Augusta National Golf Club

# Gary Player's Career Victories

## PGA Tour

1958 Kentucky Derby Open. 1959 British Open Championship. 1961 Lucky International Open, Sunshine Open Invitational, Masters Tournament. 1962 PGA Championship. 1963 San Diego Open Invitational. 1964 Pensacola Open Invitational, 500 Festival Open Invitation. 1965 U.S. Open Championship. 1968 British Open Championship. 1969 Tournament of Champions. 1970 Greater Greensboro Open. 1971 Greater Jacksonville Open, National Airlines Open Invitational. 1972 Greater New Orleans Open, PGA Championship. 1973 Southern Open. 1974 Masters Tournament, Danny Thomas Memphis Classic, British Open Championship. 1978 Masters Tournament, MONY Tournament of Champions, Houston Open.

## Champions Tour

1985 Quadel Senior Classic. 1986 General Foods PGA Seniors' Championship, United Hospitals Senior Golf Championship, Denver Post Champions of Golf. 1987 Mazda Senior Tournament Players Championship, U.S. Senior Open, PaineWebber World Seniors Invitational. 1988 General Foods PGA Seniors' Championship, Aetna Challenge, Southwestern Bell Classic, U.S. Senior Open, GTE North Classic. 1989 GTE North Classic, The RJR Championship. 1990 PGA Seniors' Championship. 1991 Royal Caribbean Classic. 1993 Bank One Classic. 1995 Bank One Classic. 1998 Northville Long Island Classic.

APPENDIX II

# INTERNATIONAL VICTORIES

1986 Nissan Senior Skins. 1987 Northville Invitational, German PGA Team Championship. 1988 Nissan Senior Skins, Senior British Open. 1990 Senior British Open. 1991 Nissan Senior Skins. 1993 Irish Senior Masters. 1997 Daiichi Seimei Cup, Senior British Open, Shell Wentworth Senior Masters. 2000 Senior Skins Game. 2009 Liberty Mutual Legends of Golf Demaret Division [with Bob Charles]. 2010 Liberty Mutual Legends of Golf Demaret Division [with Bob Charles].

# OTHER VICTORIES

1955 East Rand Open, Egyptian Matchplay. 1956 East Rand Open, South African Open, Ampol Tournament, Dunlop Tournament at Sunningdale. 1957 Western Province Open, Australian PGA Championship, Coffs Harbour Tournament. 1958 Australian Open, Natal Open, Ampol Tournament, Coffs Harbour Tournament. 1959 Transvaal Open, South African PGA Championship, Natal Open, Western Province Open, South African Masters, Victorian Open.

1960 Sprite Tournament, Transvaal Open, South African Open, South African PGA Championship, South African Masters, Natal Open, Western Province Open. 1961 Yomiuri Open, Ampol Tournament. 1962 Australian Open, Transvaal Open, Natal Open. 1963 Sponsored 5000, Liquid Air Tournament, Richelieu Grand Prix (Cape Town), Richelieu Grand Prix (Johannesburg), Australian Open, Transvaal Open, South African Masters. 1964 South African Masters. 1965 Australian Open, Piccadilly World Match Play Championship, South African Open, World Cup [indiv], World Cup [with Harold Henning], World Series of Golf, NTL Challenge Cup. 1966 Piccadilly World Match Play Championship, Transvaal Open, South African Open, Natal Open. 1967 South African Open, South African Masters. 1968 Piccadilly World Match Play Championship, World Series of Golf, South African Open. 1969 Australian Open, South African Open, South African PGA Championship, Australian Masters.

1970 Australian Open, Dunlop International. 1971 South Africa Masters, Piccadilly World Match Play Championship, General Motors Open, Western Province Open. 1972 South African Masters I, South African

Masters II, Western Province Open, Japan Airlines Open, South African Open, Brazilian Open, World Series of Golf. 1973 General Motors Open, Piccadilly World Match Play Championship. 1974 South African Masters, Rand International Open, General Motors International Classic, Ibergolf Tournament, La Manga Tournament, Australian Open, Brazilian Open. 1975 Lancome Trophy, South African Open, General Motors Classic. 1976 General Motors Open, South African Masters I, South African Masters II, South African Open. 1977 South African Open, ICL International, World Cup [indiv]. 1979 South African Open, South African PGA Championship, Kronenbrau Championship, Sun City.

1980 Chile Open, Trophy Felix Houphonet-Boigny. 1981 South African Open. Gold Coast Classic. 1982 South African PGA Championship. 1983 Skins Game. 1984 Johnnie Walker. 1986 Nissan Skins Game. 1988 Nissan Skins Game.

1991 Nissan Skins Game. 1994 Skills Challenge. 1995 Alfred Dunhill Challenge. 1997 Daiichi Seimei Cup, Nelson Mandela Invitational, South African Open.

Source: pgatour.com

# About the Author

John Boyette is sports editor of the *Augusta Chronicle*. He has covered twenty-four Masters Tournaments and has directed the newspaper's award-winning coverage since 2001. His first trip to the Masters came in 1974, and the winner that year was South Africa's Gary Player. He took up the game six years later, and he regularly plays at Palmetto Golf Club in his hometown of Aiken, South Carolina. Boyette, forty-six, has been honored by the Golf Writers Association of America and other media organizations throughout his career for his golf writing. He lives in Aiken with his wife, Kathy.

Books by John Boyette
*The 1986 Masters: How Jack Nicklaus Roared Back to Win* (2011)

Visit us at
www.historypress.net